PHILOSOPHY OF RELIGION SERIES

Editor's Note

The philosophy of religion is one of several very active branches of philosophy today, and the present series is designed both to consolidate the gains of the past and to direct attention upon the problems of the future. Between them these volumes will cover every aspect of the subject, introducing it to the reader in the state in which it is today, including its open ends and growing points. Thus the series is designed to be used as a comprehensive textbook for students. But it is also offered as a contribution to present-day discussion; and each author will accordingly go beyond the scope of an introduction to formulate his own position in the light of contemporary debates.

JOHN HICK

Philosophy of Religion Series

General Editor: John Hick, H. G. Wood Professor of Theology,
University of Birmingham

Published
John Hick (Birmingham University) Arguments
for the Existence of God
H. P. Owen (King's College, London) Concepts of Deity

Forthcoming titles
M. J. Charlesworth (Melbourne University)
Philosophy of Religion: The Historic Approaches
Terence Penelhum (Calgary University)
Problems of Religious Knowledge
Ninian Smart (Lancaster University) The Phenomenon of Religion
William C. Christian (Yale University)
Oppositions of Religious Doctrines:
An Approach to Claims of Different Religions
Basil Mitchell (Oriel College, Oxford)
The Language of Religion
Nelson Pike (California University)
Religious Experience and Mysticism
Donald Evans (Toronto University) Religion and Morality
Kai Nielsen (New York University)
Contemporary Critiques of Religion
Dennis Nineham (Keble College, Oxford) Faith and History
H. D. Lewis (King's College, London) The Self and Immortality

CONCEPTS OF DEITY

H. P. OWEN

HERDER AND HERDER

1971
HERDER AND HERDER NEW YORK
232 Madison Avenue, New York 10016

Library of Congress Catalog Card Number: 72–150307
© 1971 by H. P. Owen

Manufactured in Great Britain

Contents

Introduction

The word 'God' and its equivalents in other languages have been used in a bewildering variety of senses. Gilbert Murray illustrates the variety in the use of the Greek θεός thus:

> We shall find Parmenides telling us that God coincides with the universe, which is a sphere and immovable; Heraclitus, that God is 'day night, summer winter, war peace, satiety hunger'; Xenophanes, that God is all-seeing, all-hearing, and all mind; and as for his supposed human shape, why, if bulls and lions were to speak about God they would doubtless tell us that he was a bull or a lion. We must notice the instinctive language of the poets, using the word θεός in many subtle senses for which our word 'God' is too stiff, too personal, and too anthropomorphic. Τὸ εὐτυχεῖν 'the fact of success', is 'a god and more than a god'; τὸ γιγνώσκειν φίλους 'the thrill of recognising a friend' after long absence, is a 'god'; wine is a 'god' whose body is poured out in libation to gods; and in the unwritten law of the human conscience 'a great god liveth and groweth not old' (1).

At the one extreme the word 'God' signifies a transcendent, infinite being who is Creator and Lord of the universe. At the other extreme it is applied (as three of Murray's quotations show) to any finite entity or experience which possesses special significance or which evokes special gratitude. Between these extremes there are a large number of other usages. Sometimes men have worshipped many gods whom they have conceived as magnified human beings existing in a supra-mundane realm. At other times they have believed in one God who is identical with the world, so that 'God' and 'Nature' become interchangeable.

Furthermore, different views of God often coexist within

the same society or religion, and even within the writings of the same thinker. Thus nearly all the dominant forms of theology were represented in the Graeco-Roman world of the first century A.D. Also these forms were combined in various ways according to the syncretistic spirit of the age. Similarly, Hinduism embraces theistic, monistic and polytheistic types of religion.

Clearly, any author who sets out to write on this vast topic in a limited space is forced to be selective. There are some usages of 'God' and 'the divine' which I shall either ignore or treat with the greatest brevity. Thus I shall not examine the concept of the Supernatural in the so-called 'primitive' religions. Again, I shall discuss polytheism (in spite of its prevalence throughout the ages) only in so far as it is opposed to monotheism.

My aim is to concentrate on those forms of theology that give (or claim to give) a distinctive sense to 'God', that are capable of intellectual expansion, and that have some degree of relevance to the outlook of my readers. I have tried to cover both ancient and modern views in both the West and East. But my main emphasis is on those views which have been or still are of the greatest theoretical and practical concern to the inhabitants of the Western world in the twentieth century.

Obviously I cannot attempt to give an exhaustive account of even those theological ideas I have selected. I claim only to give an outline of them and to indicate the problems that they raise. I have concentrated on philosophical principles rather than historical detail, and I have discussed individual thinkers only for the purpose of illustrating ideas. Those who wish for further information should consult the works to which I shall refer together with the books mentioned in the select Bibliography.

Four further comments of an introductory kind are required.

1. 'God' can function in both religious and philosophical contexts. Sometimes these are separate; but they often interact in a number of different ways. I shall deal primarily with

philosophical concepts of God, and with religious concepts only in so far as they contribute to philosophical understanding.

2. In some systems of philosophical speculation another word discharges the functions that are discharged by the word 'God' in the Judaeo-Christian tradition. Thus some philosophers accord to the Absolute the metaphysical status that Christians accord to God. I shall consider it within my province to discuss such equivalents.

3. The different ideas of God I shall examine overlap at many points. Some of these points are so obvious that there will be no need for me to state them; but others call for analysis. We must also remember (as I have already remarked) that some thinkers attempt to combine opposing forms of theology within one system.

4. This book is a study in ontology — in the being and nature of God. Yet one cannot completely separate ontology from epistemology — the question of being from the question of knowledge; for it is always necessary to ask how one knows that God exists and that he has this or that character. Hence I shall be obliged to touch on epistemological matters, although I must leave a full discussion of them to other writers in this series.

The plan of this book is as follows. In Chapter 1 I shall discuss classical theism. In Chapter 2 I shall discuss four main other forms of theology — the idea of a finite God, the Neo-Platonic concept of God, pantheism and process theology. In Chapter 3 I shall discuss the thought of six twentieth-century thinkers — Pringle-Pattison, Barth, Brunner, Radhakrishnan, Tillich and John Macquarrie. After much deliberation I have chosen these on the following grounds. Pringle-Pattison's Gifford Lectures (which constitute the most substantial book written explicitly on the idea of God in English during this century) is significant for its attempt to mediate between theism and monism. Barth and Brunner are the two most influential Christian dogmatic theologians of this century. Radhakrishnan merits attention both because he is among the two or three most distinguished

Indian thinkers of his generation, and because he is supreme among those who have tried to unite the thought-forms of the East and West. Tillich is included on account of the notice which his writings have attracted in recent years. Macquarrie is the most important representative of existentialist theology in the English-speaking world. I have not included a Roman Catholic theologian solely because the characteristic theology of the Roman Catholic Church is identical with the classical theism that I shall examine in Chapter 1. As far as possible I shall relate my critiques of these thinkers to the analyses given in Chapters 1 and 2.

I have devoted more space to the theistic form than to non-theistic forms of religious belief (to Chapter 1 than to Chapter 2) for two reasons. First, the theistic form is the one that has exercised the greatest influence on Western civilisation in general and Western philosophy in particular. Consequently when anyone in the West is asked 'Do you believe in God?' he assumes that the questioner means the God of Christianity. My second reason (which, of course, would be insufficient if it were not supported by the first) is that I am, by both upbringing and conviction, a Christian theist. And it is proper to speak most copiously of matters with which one is directly acquainted.

However, the second of these reasons raises the question of impartiality. The simple answer to this question is that, although we cannot avoid having presuppositions, we can do our best to avoid having irrational prejudices — that is, either a prejudice against submitting our presuppositions to rational scrutiny or a prejudice which prevents us from distinguishing between good and bad reasons for adhering to our presuppositions. I can only say that although I cannot divest myself of presuppositions I have done my best to divest myself of prejudice; that if theistic presuppositions can cause prejudice, so also can non-theistic ones; but that the achievement of objectivity lies within the ability of anyone who regards it as being of supreme importance.

I fully realise that the preceding paragraph implies that the human mind is capable of reflecting meaningfully on the Supernatural, and that this capacity is denied by many philosophers today. The validation of this capacity falls outside my scope. I can only hope that, so far as this book is concerned, faith in theological metaphysics will be justified by its works.

Chapter 1

(a) Classical theism (1)

Theism may be defined as belief in one God, the Creator, who is infinite, self-existent, incorporeal, eternal, immutable, impassible, simple, perfect, omniscient and omnipotent. I shall examine each element in this definition according to the order I have given. But first I must say something concerning the historical origins of theism.

So far as the Western world is concerned, theism has a double origin: the Bible and Greek philosophy. All the divine properties I named in the preceding paragraph are implied in the Bible; but the expression and, still more, the amplification of them were due to the influence of Greek philosophy. Attempts to present Scriptural revelation through philosophical concepts had been made by Jews of the Diaspora (1) before any book of the New Testament was written. Thus Philo (*c.* 20 B.C.-*c.* A.D. 50) described God in highly abstract, metaphysical language that (apart from references to the Scriptures) could have come from a pagan Platonist. Diasporate Jews found it necessary to reformulate the Scriptural view of God philosophically in order first to make it fully intelligible to themselves, secondly to communicate with Gentiles, and thirdly to show that the idea of God contained in their Scriptures was fully compatible with the best non-Jewish thought of their day. For the same reasons Christian theologians from the beginning of the second century wrote of God in terms designed to satisfy the demands of philosophical speculation.

The philosophical presentation of theology (by which I mean the basic theory of God's nature) was begun by the Apologists (2) and continued by both the ante- and post-Nicene Fathers (3). It reached its climax in the writings of the two great theologians St Augustine (354-430) and St

Thomas Aquinas (*c.* 1225-74). Above all it was Aquinas who systematised and gave authoritative form to this lengthy and complex process of reflection. Consequently I shall take the works of Aquinas — and especially his 'Summa Theologica' — as the chief source for classical theism (4). But of course I shall consider other writers. Also I shall not refer, still less imply assent, to everything that Aquinas says. My intention is simply to use him as the supreme exponent of the view I am discussing.

Before proceeding to detailed exposition I must clarify the relation between classical theism and Judaeo-Christian revelation.

Classical theism (as I have defined it) can be called 'Christian' on at least four grounds. First, it arose within the context of orthodox belief in Biblical revelation. Secondly, although there are extensive parallels to many aspects of Christian theism in the writings of non-Jewish and non-Christian philosophers in the ancient world, there are some aspects that seem to be unparalleled. Thus it is very hard to find a clear and consistent parallel to the Christian idea of God as one who creates the world *ex nihilo,* or to the Christian idea of him as one who is both infinite and fully personal. Thirdly, even where there are parallels there is nothing in any non-Christian source that is philosophically comparable to the statements of theism given by Aquinas and those Christian thinkers who are directly or indirectly indebted to him. Fourthly (and consequently), throughout the Christian era non-Christian philosophers, as well as Christian ones, have almost always discussed theism in one or other of its Christian formulations.

In order to complete this summary of the background, it is necessary to make three distinctions.

(a) One must distinguish between those elements in the Christian idea of God which do and those which do not depend intrinsically on Biblical revelation. I shall be concerned almost wholly with those elements which do not thus depend. In fact no element in the definition of theism I gave is necessarily thus dependent. But occasionally I shall refer to doctrines (chiefly those of the Trinity and the Incarnation)

2

which are necessarily linked to the (supposedly) revelatory events from which they took their origin.

(b) One must distinguish between the meaning of a theistic statement and the grounds for believing in the existence of the God to whom the statement refers. Such a statement can be meaningful (perhaps in a variety of senses) even if there are no grounds (or no adequate grounds) for assenting to its existential truth. Obviously the question of meaning and the question of grounds overlap; but I am concerned mainly with the first question; so that, although I shall inevitably touch on the second, I must leave a full treatment of it to other writers in this series.

(c) One must distinguish between the grounds for believing in God's existence and the grounds for preferring one concept of God to another. Once again, there is overlapping. Yet I shall be concerned mainly with the second type of ground. My task is not to answer the question: 'What grounds (if any) are there for supposing that God exists?' But it falls within my province to attempt an answer to the question: 'What grounds (if any) are there for preferring one concept of God to another?'

In fact, I believe that theism is preferable to any non-theistic view of God on grounds of reason, revelation and experience. Yet so far as this book is concerned my use of these grounds is purely hypothetical. The most I can claim to show — and I hope that my analysis will show this much — is that *if* God exists the theistic view of him is intrinsically more rational (or reasonable) than any other; that *if* the Christian claim to a distinctive revelation is valid such a revelation can be regarded as being fully congruous with the theistic (as it is not with any non-theistic) view; and that *if* religious experience is genuinely cognitive it is most satisfactorily interpreted in terms of theism. But I do not claim to remove the 'ifs'. Whether reason can prove God's existence, whether the Christian claim to have received a special revelation is true (or even rationally defensible), and whether religious experience in any of its forms is cognitive — these are questions that fall outside my scope. All my references to the theistic proofs, to revelation and to religious experience

3

must be interpreted within this hypothetical framework.

Having, I trust, made clear my criteria of analysis and evaluation, I shall proceed to examine in detail the definition of classical theism I have given.

1. *The unity of God.* To Western man throughout the history of Christendom the unity of God has been taken for granted. But polytheism prevailed throughout the Graeco-Roman world in which Christianity arose. People of all intellectual and moral types believed in many gods (both in the members of the ancient Olympic pantheon and in the newer deities of the mystery cults). Even those philosophers (such as Plato and the Stoics) who imply monotheism in some passages, are uninhibitedly polytheistic in others; they can even use 'God' and 'the gods' interchangeably in the same passage without any explanation.

Monotheism arose gradually in the religion of Israel. Scholars still dispute when exactly it first appeared; but it was certainly affirmed in the sixth century by the so-called 'Second Isaiah' (5); and it quickly became an unquestioned axiom of Jewish theology. Hence it was taken for granted by St Paul, who opposed to the many gods of the pagan world the one God of Judaeo-Christian revelation (6). The unity of God remained a primary item in Christian apologetic of the second and third centuries.

There are three possible grounds for affirming God's unity: revelation, experience and reason. Theistic belief must in fact always be justified on one or other of these grounds, which overlap and intermingle in many ways.

The first of these grounds is obvious. The Jews affirmed the existence of one God (Yahweh), not on the score of abstract speculation, but because they believed that Yahweh had thus revealed himself to them throughout their history, and especially in the pivotal events of the Exodus and the Exile. According to the New Testament this self-disclosure of the one, true God was fulfilled in Christ — both in his teaching on the Father and in his person as the Father's only Son.

The second ground consists, not in the mere fact of
4

religious experience (which has taken polytheistic forms), but in an inference from the experience's subjective aspect to its putative object. The inference runs thus. If the divine is to be the object of absolute devotion it must possess absolute being; but one among many gods cannot possess such being, for he shares his nature with other gods; therefore the divine must be one. I shall recur to another more pointed and (I think) persuasive form of this argument in discussing God's self-existence.

Lastly, philosophers have attempted to demonstrate God's unity by pure reason. Aquinas states the demonstration thus. I shall quote the passage in full because it is an excellent example of his style (and so of theistic reasoning):

That there is one God can be shown in three ways.

First, because God is simple. For clearly no individual can share with others its very singularity. Socrates can share what makes him man with many others, but what makes him this man can belong to one alone. So if Socrates were this man just by being a man, there could no more be many men than there can be many Socrates. Now in God this is the case, for as we showed God is himself his own nature. So to be God is to be this God. And it is thus impossible for there to be many Gods.

Secondly, because God's perfection is unlimited. For God, as we have seen, embraces in himself the whole perfection of existence. Now many Gods, if they existed, would have to differ. Something belonging to one would not belong to the other. And if this were a lack the one God would not be altogether perfect, whilst if it were a perfection the other God would lack it. So there cannot be more than one God. And this is why philosophers in ancient times, bowing, so to speak, to the truth, held that if the source of things was unlimited it could not be many.

Thirdly, because the world is one. For we find all existent things in mutual order, certain of them subserving others. Now divers things only combine in a single order where there is a single cause of order. For unity and order is introduced into a plurality of things more perfectly by a single cause than by many, unity producing unity essentially whilst the many produce unity only incidentally in so far as they too are somehow one. So the primary source of unity and order in the universe, namely, God, must be one himself, for the primary is always most perfect and not incidental but essential (7).

The first and second of these arguments are sound if their premises are granted. If God is his own nature or essence he cannot share his nature with anyone else (as Socrates can share his nature with other men). Similarly, if God is infinite, or unlimited, he must be one; for if there were many gods, one god, lacking forms of deity that the others possessed, would be to that extent imperfect and limited. Here we have two simple deductive proofs of God's unity.

Aquinas's third 'proof' is dubitable. It may be questioned (a) whether the universe constitutes a single order, (b) whether such order as we discover in the universe demands a transcendent explanation, and (c) whether we need postulate a *single* Orderer. I cannot consider these questions here; for to do so would involve a thorough discussion of the teleological argument (8); but it is clear that the third of Aquinas's arguments for divine unity does not have the logical self-evidence of his first and second arguments.

However, the first and second of the arguments rest on the premises that God's essence and existence are identical, and that he is infinite. Aquinas has claimed to establish the truth of these premises previously in his 'Summa'; and I shall examine them shortly. My excuse for thus anticipating the development of classical (specifically Thomist) theism is triple. First, my whole discussion — my every use of the word 'God' — presupposes divine unity. Secondly, however obvious God's unity may seem to us, it was by no means obvious to Plato (not to mention a host of lesser pre-Christian thinkers). Thirdly, the passage I quoted from Aquinas exemplifies, not only the power and precision of his mind, but also his determination to base even undisputed axioms of Christian theology as far as possible on reason.

Christians, moreover, believe, not merely that God is one,

6

but also that he is three-in-one. In this they depart from the undiluted monotheism of Judaism and Islam. The doctrine of the Trinity cannot be adequately treated here. I wish only to state four points which are necessary for a minimal understanding of it.

1. The doctrine is not a piece of *a priori* speculation. In this it differs from Plotinus's theory of the One, Mind and Soul (9). It is grounded in the historical revelation recorded in the New Testament. The Fathers evolved the doctrine on the basis of those Scriptural passages in which the one God of Israel revealed himself in the three distinct forms of Father, Son and Holy Spirit.

2. In formulating the doctrine of the Trinity, orthodox theologians are obliged to steer a *via media* between tritheism (the affirmation of three gods) and modalism (the view that the three are merely different aspects of an undifferentiated unity). On the one hand they must preserve the unity of God. On the other hand they must devise a formulation that reflects an objective distinction between the members of the Triad. The formula at which the Fathers ultimately arrived is that God exists as one substance (*substantia, οὐσία*) in three persons (*personae, ὑπόστασεις*).

3. This formula was not meant to be an adequate description of the Godhead. If (to anticipate my discussion of 'transcendence') God is incomprehensible even when he is considered as a unity, he must *a fortiori* be so when he is considered as a triunity. Every finite analogy (such as the psychological analogy of three faculties existing in one human soul, or the social analogy of three human persons belonging to one family) is bound to be inadequate. It can finally do no more than point to a unique form of being that must remain a mystery.

4. The doctrine affirms that God is both self-sufficient and loving. At first sight these properties seem to be mutually exclusive; for in so far as love implies a need for the object loved it appears to be incompatible with self-sufficiency. The doctrine of the Trinity overcomes this apparent incompatibility by affirming that God's own self-sufficient life is itself a life of love. God exists through the mutual love that

7

binds together his single nature as Father, Son and Holy Spirit.

If, then, God is infinite and self-existent he must be one. If, too, he has revealed himself as existing in three distinct forms he must also be three-in-one. But the two 'ifs' remain. I cannot here attempt to remove the second; for to do so would involve a complete examination of distinctively Christian truth-claims. I shall, however, attempt to remove the first 'if' — at any rate to the extent of giving the theistic reasons for postulating God's infinity and self-existence. But before I deal with these two concepts I must discuss the belief that the one God is the Creator of all things.

2. *God the Creator.* According to classical theism God created the world 'out of nothing' (*ex nihilo*). Two things must be noted concerning the phrase *ex nihilo*. First, it is analytic, not synthetic. It does not add anything to the idea of creation; it merely makes the idea explicit. Secondly, 'nothing' is to be taken in the strict sense of absolute non-being or non-existence. There is no form of being that exists apart from God's creative act. Everything depends absolutely on him for its very being.

The idea of creation is thus radically opposed to the non-theistic views of God that I shall examine in Chapter 2. It is opposed to the view held in the ancient world by Plato, and in the modern world by A. N. Whitehead, that God imposes form on pre-existent matter. It is opposed to the Plotinian theory that the world is the last in a series of emanations from the Godhead. Still more obviously it is opposed to pantheism (according to which the world is either identical with God or in some way a self-expression of his nature).

The doctrine of creation cannot be fully understood unless the following points are borne in mind.

(a) The contrast between the creature and the Creator must be distinguished from the contrast between appearance and reality. The created world is in no sense unreal. It is fully real according to the limits which it has received from the Creator. A created world *cannot* be merely an apparent (and so an illusory) one; for the only reality of which it could be

8

an appearance is God; but the whole point of the creature — Creator contrast is to affirm that the world and God are ontologically distinct.

Admittedly Aquinas said that finite entities possess varied degrees of being in relation to God, who is 'the most fully in being (*maxime ens*)'. But although creatures possess being to the extent that they reflect their self-existent Source (so that one has more being than another) they all *really* possess the degree of being that their natures are capable of exercising. Thus although a worm occupies a low place in the scale of created being, it really is a worm (and not a part of God's dream or a peripheral element in his cosmic self-expression).

(b) Although the world totally depends on God it has what may be called a 'relative independence' or 'derived autonomy'. In creating the world God endowed it with its own principles of operation, which are therefore intelligible in their own right. Thus we can explain the behaviour of physical objects through those laws that are discovered by the natural sciences. Again, we can explain human behaviour partly through physical and psychological laws, but partly too (so theists maintain) through the fact of free will.

It has been objected that the idea of creation is incompatible with the idea of free will. Antony Flew puts the objection thus: 'As Creator he [God] must be first cause, prime mover, supporter, and controller of every thought and action throughout his utterly dependent universe. In short: if creation is in, autonomy is out' (10). Flew is here guilty of a glaring paralogism. The idea of creation does not entail the view that the Creator 'controls every thought'. God can create such beings as he wills; and in fact he has chosen to create some beings with a capacity for free choice.

(c) Although God is, ontologically, the first cause of everything (in so far as everything depends on his creative *fiat*), he normally operates entirely through secondary causes — that is, through the laws of nature and human free will.

(d) We cannot isolate God's primary causality and observe it. It is wholly hidden in the secondary causes that it animates. It can be apprehended only by a distinctively metaphysical act of reason or faith.

9

(e) Nevertheless, since God is the Creator he can intervene by an immediate supernatural act in the normal processes of creation if such an intervention is compatible with both his own nature and the nature of the created entities concerned. If finite entities are essentially dependent on God they must be open to any possible effects that he chooses to create in them. I can only state this basic principle. I must leave a detailed discussion of miracles to others.

(f) The world depends on God *continuously* for its existence. Deists of the eighteenth century held that God, having made the world 'at the beginning,' left it to continue on its own according to the laws that he imparted to it. Admittedly this view is supported by a literalistic interpretation of the creation myths in Genesis; but it is now widely agreed that the latter are to be taken as symbolical statements of a permanent relation between God and the world; and such a relation is implied by Biblical teaching as a whole. It is in any case self-evident that if (as theists have consistently maintained) the world is wholly dependent on God it must be thus dependent throughout its history; for if it is wholly dependent it would immediately cease to be if God's creative power were withdrawn. Absolute dependence cannot, logically, have limits. Hence from the divine standpoint creation and preservation are identical.

(g) Consequently theism is unaffected by scientific cosmology. To put it with inevitable over-simplicity, some cosmologists hold that the universe arose from an initial (and roughly datable) explosion in an initial state of matter; but others hold that the universe has existed for an infinite duration. Belief in God's creativity is compatible with both these theories. It would not be compatible with the second theory if God's creativity were restricted to an initial moment of time; but if it is not thus restricted it can be extended to whatever duration the universe possesses. Such an extension admittedly implies that God himself has no temporal beginning. But the belief that God has no beginning or end is a minimal element in the concept of his eternity — a concept that I shall examine later.

(h) God's creative act has no finite parallel. No human
10

person can create anything *ex nihilo*. Thus the so-called 'creative' artist always works on given material — words, paint, stone. Even the purest of arts, music, presupposes a bodily instrument and its tonal potentialities. Furthermore every artist is a human person. And every human person is, not humanly created *ex nihilo*, but (as we significantly say) *pro*-created by his parents from their genetic material.

(i) Consequently, God's creativity is bound to be incomprehensible. We can form analogies to it; but none of these is an exact parallel; they point (when qualified) to an act that is different in kind from any of which we have direct experience, and that is therefore bound to elude our understanding.

This incomprehensibility becomes especially apparent when we consider *why* God creates the world. Here we seem to be confronted with the following antinomy. If we say that God creates by a free act of will we imply that God might not have created, or even that he was reluctant to create; but there are reasons (which I shall examine shortly) for holding that all God's acts are necessary expressions of his nature, and we cannot square divine love with any reluctance to give. Yet if we say that God creates 'of necessity', do we not imply that God needs the world for the completion of his being, so that he cannot be (as theists affirm that he is) self-sufficient?

The theistic solution of this antinomy is to affirm on the one hand that God's creative act is free in so far as it is neither externally constrained nor necessary for the fulfilment of his own life, but on the other hand that it is a necessary *consequence* of the self-sufficient life of love that he enjoys within his triune Godhead. We can partly understand this necessity in so far as even we are capable of doing good to others without expecting, or even needing, good from them in return. Yet we cannot entirely understand it; for all our altruistic deeds in fact help to complete our moral natures, although we do not perform them for the sake of this completion.

(j) However, although we cannot comprehend either the nature of or the motive for God's creative act, our postulation of this act is entirely rational; for we can at least see

11

that it represents to a supreme degree a power and a love that we experience only in restricted modes. Because God is self-sufficient he can exert creative power absolutely. Also because he is self-sufficient he alone can exhibit love in a form that is *wholly* altruistic.

The grounds for accepting the doctrine of creation are constituted by the usual triad: reason, revelation and experience. The cosmological argument states that if we are to have a sufficient reason for, or ultimate explanation of, the world we must postulate self-existent Being as its creative source. That God creates the word *ex nihilo* is implied throughout the New Testament (which, by general agreement, is the primary source of Christian revelation). The clearest statement is in the Johannine prologue, where it is said of the divine and pre-existent Word that 'all things were made through him'. The experiential ground is the sense of dependence which Schleiermacher regarded as the core of religion and to which the Bible everywhere testifies.

3. *Divine infinity.* It is necessary to begin by stating three things that 'infinity' does *not* mean in classical theism. First, it does not mean that God is shapeless or formless. On the contrary he is (in terms of the Aristotelian contrast) pure Form; for there is no composition in his being. I shall amplify this statement later. Secondly, to say that God is infinite is not to say that he is characterless. He has the character of pure Spirit.

These erroneous interpretations of divine infinity are especially apt to occur when we think of it by means of the sensory imagination. We so easily imagine 'the infinite' as a shapeless and indeterminate mass (or, perhaps, empty space). Here, as elsewhere, we must remember that God is wholly incorporeal; so that, although we cannot rid our minds completely of sense-images in thinking of him, we must ultimately negate all those properties of being that are applicable only to material entities.

Thirdly, and in particular, we must not think of God's infinity as an infinite extension of merely human attributes. To this view there are several objections. It would be

12

incompatible with the ascription of a fixed character to God; for there would always be a yet further point to which human attributes could be extended. It would be self-contradictory; for the very idea of a human person involves the idea of a being who is limited in relation to other beings of the same species (and, of course, to all the other items in the universe). It would be religiously offensive; for it would make God out to be merely a magnified man who differs in degree, but not in kind, from his creatures.

The 'in' in 'infinite' is to be taken as a negative prefix. It means that God is non-finite. In order to arrive at a true notion of him we must deny to him all those limitations that affect created being. Therefore we very often need to use negative predicates (such as 'immutable') to express his infinity. But we can also use positive ones, provided they are properly interpreted. Thus God's 'simplicity' means his complete expression of all his attributes in all his acts.

There is little more that can be profitably said about God's infinity as such; for merely to say that he is non-finite, or non-limited, is to offer only a minimal basis for theism. Let us, therefore, consider the forms of being in which God's infinity is expressed.

4. *Divine self-existence.* The primary and all-determinative sign of God's infinity is his self-existence. The limited nature of each created entity is shown primarily in the fact of its dependence. Let us take the existence of me (the writer) and you (the reader). Each of us is dependent on innumerable factors of both a physical and a mental kind in both the past and the present. Without the past factors we should not have come into being, and without the present factors we should not remain in being. Neither of us contains within himself the reason for his existence.

God, however, is self-existent. He does not depend upon any external factors for his being. He is wholly self-sufficient. His self-existence or self-sufficiency is the primary point of difference between him and his finite creatures. Correlatively it is the primary mark of his infinity, as Aquinas remarks: 'The very fact that God's existence itself subsists without

13

being acquired by anything, and as such is limitless (*prout dicitur infinitum*), distinguishes it from everything else, and sets other things aside from it' (11).

God's self-existence can be expressed through three further categories.

(a) Whereas creatures exist *per se* ('by or in themselves'), only the Creator exists *a se* ('from or of himself'). To say that creatures exist *per se* is to affirm (against monism) that each of them is real, distinct and autonomous. Yet their autonomy is limited; and the principal form of limitation is their dependence on external factors. God's total independence of such factors, and his consequently total self-sufficiency, are sometimes expressed by saying that he alone exists *a se* (or that he alone possesses *aseitas*).

(b) We can also state God's self-existence by saying that in him essence and existence are identical. In every finite being essence and existence, though inseparable, are distinct. Let us first approach the matter from the standpoint of essence. It is not true of any finite entity that its essence (*what* it is) is identical with its existence (*that* it is). Let us take the case of a man – John. Even if we had a complete description of, or insight into, John's nature we should still not have a complete account of his existence; his nature would not explain his existence; we could still ask 'What causes him to be?' In the case of God, however, there is no such distinction between his nature and his being. If we could fully grasp his nature, or essence, we should see it as pervaded by a power of inevitable existence. Correlatively one can say that God's existence is identical with his essence. The existence of every finite entity is limited by its essence or nature; so that it is a mode or determination of being. Thus John is a man (in contrast with an animal), and an individual man (in contrast with other men). But God's existence is not thus limited by his nature. There is no form of being that he does not express fully and simultaneously.

There are two objections that may be raised here. It may be said that God is limited first by the fact that he is incorporeal (and so cannot express corporeal being), and secondly by the fact that his being does not include the finite

14

world (so that all modes of finite being are excluded from his life). These are only apparent limitations. God, on the contrary, would be limited if he *was* corporeal; for corporeal attributes are intrinsically limiting. Similarly he would be limited if he *did* include the world in either its spiritual or its material aspects; for the existence of everything in the world is limited by its dependence on other things, and ultimately by its dependence on God as its Creator.

(c) God's self-existence can also be stated through the affirmation that he exists 'necessarily', or that he is a 'necessary' being (*ens necessarium*). Yet if this affirmation is to be truly understood, three things must be remembered.

First, we must distinguish between relative and absolute necessity. If we believe (*contra* Hume) that causal sequences are objectively necessitated we must assert that everything is necessary in so far as it is caused. But its necessity is entirely relative to its causes, which in turn are necessitated by other causes. God alone is absolutely necessary; for he alone contains the necessity of existing within his own being.

Secondly, 'necessity' in this context has an ontological, not a logical, significance; it refers to God's existence, not to propositions concerning his existence. Moreover, ontological does not entail logical necessity. There is no inconsistency in both affirming that God's existence is necessary and denying (as I should deny) that the affirmation of his existence is logically necessary (or conceptually inevitable). This vital distinction is stated thus by A. C. A. Rainer in a reply to J. N. Findlay:

> The necessity of God's existence is not the same as the necessity of a logical implication. It means, for those who believe in it, God's complete actuality, indestructibility, *aseitas* or independence of limiting conditions. It is a property ascribed to God, not a property of our assertions about God. To maintain that the ascription of such a property is logically absurd is to confuse the necessity of God's Being with the necessity of our thinking about it. That is to commit the converse fallacy of Anselm's ontological argument, namely, to say that a Perfect Being

15

cannot exist necessarily, because we cannot necessarily assert its existence. Our assertion of God's existence may be contingent, although God's existence is necessary in the sense of being indestructible or eternal (12).

Lastly, God's necessity is bound to be incomprehensible. We cannot form any positive idea of it, for it has no kind of parallel in finite experience. We can offer finite analogies (inadequate though they are) to many of God's attributes; but there is no analogy to his self-existence. Here we can strictly speak of him as 'the wholly Other' who is 'absolutely unique', and who therefore constitutes an impenetrable mystery for finite minds.

Nevertheless, the affirmation of divine necessity is not self-contradictory. Those who accuse it of being so make one or both of two unwarranted assumptions. They assume either that necessity must characterise propositions (and never things) or that God is a magnified finite entity to whom the attribute of necessity is arbitrarily affixed. The first of these assumptions is a sheer *petitio principii*; for the fact that all finite beings are contingent does not rule out the possibility that there is an infinite being whose distinguishing mark is his necessity. With reference to the second assumption it is enough to repeat that God's infinity is to be construed, not as an extrapolation from notions of creaturely being, but as freedom from those factors that condition and circumscribe both the nature and the existence of creatures.

The grounds for postulating God's self-existence are, inevitably, those to which I have already referred. First, there is the purely rational ground stated in the cosmological argument. Only a self-existent God constitutes a sufficient reason for the world. If God were finite he would be simply one among the innumerable items in the world; so that we could ask 'What caused him?', just as we can ask 'What caused them?' Was he caused by another 'god' (and so on *ad infinitum*)? Clearly, we can have an *ultimate* explanation of *all* finite entities only in a God who transcends the finite series altogether.

The experiential ground for postulating his self-existence
16

consists, not in the mere fact of religious experience, but in an argument from the latter in its strongest form. The argument (which is surely irrefutable) is that we cannot offer complete worship — complete adoration and self-commitment — to a God who is merely *primus inter pares* and perishable. God must be unique and imperishable; but he cannot be so unless he is infinite and self-existent.

Admittedly the ground in Biblical revelation is not so obvious. The Biblical writers do not explicitly affirm God's self-existence, for they did not have the requisite interest in metaphysical reflection; but they imply it in stating that God is the Creator of all that is, and that he is the fitting object of absolute worship. Above all they imply it in their pre-supposition of God's ultimacy. They took it for granted that there *cannot* be anything beyond God. Hence the interpretation of the divine name as 'He Who Is' was found to be inevitable.

All the divine attributes that I shall proceed to examine are entailed by, and therefore (so far as classical theism is concerned) must be interpreted through, the idea of God's infinity or self-existence. If God is infinite or self-existent being he must be incorporeal (for matter is intrinsically limiting), eternal (for the present of every temporal being is limited by its past and future), immutable (for change implies a defect of being), impassible (at least in the sense that God cannot suffer any change from either an internal or an external cause), simple (for his whole nature is actualised in all he is and does), perfect (for any imperfection in his nature would be also an imperfection in his being), omniscient (in the sense that all his cognitive powers must be actualised), and omnipotent (in the sense that all his volitional powers also must be actualised).

(b) Classical theism (2)

5. *Divine incorporeality.* It is obvious that matter in general, and the material body in particular, are intrinsically limiting. Everything that exists in space inevitably excludes

17

other things that occupy other portions of space. Therefore if God is infinite he must be non-spatial and bodiless. He must be *pure* Spirit.

God's incorporeality can also be proved from his self-existence, which (it must always be remembered) is the primary mark of his infinity. No material entity can be self-existent; for each is a determination, or mode, of being. Consequently we can always ask of any such entity: 'What are its causes and conditions?'

It is sometimes objected that the ideal of incorporeal being is meaningless (perhaps self-contradictory). Whether we find it so depends on our antecedent view of the human mind's relation to its body. If we hold that mental activities are identical with, or modes of, physical ones we have no analogy to pure Spirit. But if we hold that our minds are onto-logically distinct from our bodies we have such an analogy. Even though we always find human minds joined to bodies, and even if the body (particularly the brain) is a condition of mental acts in our present state, we can reasonably postulate the existence of a Mind from which this conjunction and condition is absent.

Here I both agree and disagree with I. M. Crombie's argument in 'Faith and Logic' (pp. 57-62). I agree with his assertions that mind is distinct from matter, and that this distinctness gives us a reference-range for the application of spirituality in a pure form to God. But I disagree with him when he proceeds to affirm that the application involves a category-mistake; for if (as he admits) mental terms are irreducible to physical ones they must (*contra* Ryle) con-stitute a separate category. Hence there is nothing logically improper in postulating the existence of a Spirit who is wholly bodiless.

I cannot here validate the belief in the ontological distinct-ness of mind. But unless it can be validated we have no basis for affirming pure spirituality in God. If the human mind is not a distinct form of being and activity we cannot give our affirmation of divine incorporeality any 'reference-range'. Here is a crucial example of the truth that theism depends on metaphysical assertions concerning the finite order.

18

Moreover, if a dualistic view of mind and matter is correct we can see, not only that God's pure spirituality is possible, but also that it is the most perfect form of being. All human behaviour approaches perfection to the extent that it expresses wisdom, goodness and love. Yet although the body aids these spiritual properties in so far as it offers a medium for their expression, it also inhibits them in many — and some tragically frustrating — ways. Hence only pure Spirit can constitute an absolutely perfect form of personal existence.

6. *Divine eternity*. The adjective 'eternal' can have two senses: 'everlasting' and 'timeless'. The first sense can be given either a strong or weak form. According to the strong form, the entity so designated always has existed and always will exist. According to the weak form, although the entity had a beginning it will have no end. The weak form is the one that is employed in Christian statements of human immortality. Every human soul is temporal in the sense that it had a beginning; but it is eternal in the sense that it will never end. Yet it is the strong form that theists have always used with reference to God — a form perfectly exemplified in Psalm 90:2: 'Before the mountains were brought forth, or ever thou hadst formed the earth and the world, from everlasting to everlasting thou art God.'

However, classical theists have held that it is not sufficient to say that God is everlasting. God, they affirm, is outside any temporal series; he is wholly timeless. The equation of eternity with timelessness was derived from Plato. It was definitively formulated by Boethius thus: *aeternitas est interminabilis vitae tota simul et perfecta possessio* ('eternity is the instantaneously whole and perfect possession of unending life') (13). Aquinas quotes these words as a definition of God's eternity. He adds that when Biblical writers describe God in terms of temporal succession they do so 'metaphorically' (14).

It is surely clear that (as Aquinas maintains) the affirmation of God's infinity and self-existence entails the affirmation of his timelessness or simultaneity. If God were

19

temporal (albeit endlessly so) his present (like every human present) would be limited by his past and future. Correspondingly, he could not be self-existent; for his being at t2 would exclude his being at t1 and t3. To put it otherwise, if God were temporal his essence would not be identical with existence; for there would always be forms of being that he has lost, and forms that he is yet to achieve. To put it in yet another way, if God were temporal we could always ask: 'What causes him to be as he is now?' In answering this question we should have to proceed *ad infinitum* in a description of his preceding states; but no such description could be final; so that God's existence would be no less contingent — no less a matter of ultimately inexplicable 'brute fact' — than the existence of the world. Therefore if God is a necessary being he must exist in a timeless present.

Two main objections can be brought against the idea of divine simultaneity.

First, it has been said that the idea of a timeless personality is meaningless. Admittedly it is meaningless in the sense that we cannot attach an adequate, positive meaning to it. But it is not meaningless in the sense of being an obvious contradiction. 'Personal' does not exclude 'timeless' (as it excludes 'impersonal', or as 'timeless' excludes 'temporal'). The charge of self-contradiction needs to be proved; it cannot rest on the assertion of conceptual opposites.

What the charge amounts to is simply this. All our mental states and acts are temporally conditioned. All our thoughts, volitions and desires take time; they are all performed in the present with reference to the past and the future. Yet why should we assume that they could not occur non-temporally? Admittedly it is not always easy to decide what is and what is not an essential property of X, or (correlatively) what can and what cannot be predicated of X without contradiction. But at least 'A mental act can be non-temporal' is not equivalent to 'The same entity is both mental and non-mental' or 'The same object is both round and square'. The law of contradiction immediately excludes the second and third statements; but it does not thus exclude the first. It could exclude the first only if we knew a non-temporal mode

20

of being, and if we knew that it cannot be compatible with a mental mode; but we do not possess either form of knowledge.

It can be reasonably claimed that temporality, so far from being a necessary condition, is a limitation of personal activity. The fact that we need to acquire knowledge in successive stages restricts the nature of our knowing. Similarly the fact that we need to act with reference to our fixed past and our uncertain future restricts the nature of our willing. The perfect case of knowing would be one in which all things were instantaneously present and fully intelligible, either as actualities or as possibilities, to the mind of the knower. Similarly the perfect case of willing would be one in which all the energies of the self were concentrated in single, simultaneous affirmation.

Furthermore there are limited analogies even within human experience to God's timelessness. Thus every human person transcends time through memory and foresight. This transcendence is a primary mark of man's superiority to sub-human creatures. Again, there are special moments of mental concentration in which all our energies are brought to bear on an object (on a problem that we are trying to solve, on a friend whom we wish to help, on God to whom we bring ourselves in prayer). In such moments both the past and the future are sharply focused in the present. Finally, there are those experiences in which we are not aware of time's passage (as when we are enjoying a work of music, or when a lover is in the presence of his beloved).

I wish to stress that these are only analogies. As finite beings we never wholly transcend temporality. Thus however much we may concentrate on a problem our concentration occupies a definite length of time. Again, although we may not be aware that a symphony has taken thirty minutes, a glance at the clock shows that it has done so. Nevertheless such experiences (which, let us note, are among the most significant ones we enjoy) point to the possibility of a self-consciousness that is wholly timeless. In Crombie's terminology, they give a 'reference-range' for the concept of divine eternity.

The second objection is more serious. It may be said that it is self-contradictory to affirm that a timeless God is the Creator of a temporal world. This objection can, I think, be met by the following observations.

(a) We must distinguish between God's act in creating the world and the world itself. It would be a sheer contradiction to assert that God includes the temporal world if he is timeless (quite as much as it would be to assert that the same physical object is blue and red all over). But theism is based on the affirmation that God and the world are ontologically distinct. God's creative act never merges with the entities it creates. Theists do not posit (as pantheists and panentheists posit) mutually exclusive properties within the Godhead itself.

(b) Although time is opposed to eternity, the former is structurally related to the latter in the order of copy to archetype; but there is no such relationship between simple sense-qualities. Time, as Plato put it, is 'a moving image of eternity' (15). In theistic terms, the world is a finite diversification through time of properties and ideas that exist infinitely, simply and simultaneously in God. The very nature of the world *qua* temporal (no less than *qua* finite and diversified) is to be a created reflection of its uncreated Ground.

(c) There is, once again, a limited analogy within finite experience to God's timeless act in creating a temporal world. A creative artist can see 'in a flash' a work (a play, a piece of music) which it will take many minutes, or even hours, to perform. I hasten to add that this is only the merest pointer to God's timeless act of creativity; for the artist's 'flash' of insight occupies *some* length of time, and the temporal gap between the insight and the performance remains. Nevertheless, the artist achieves a limited transcendence over time. If we could (as we cannot) imagine his insight as being absolutely timeless and being endowed with a simultaneous power of enactment we should have reached the infinite case of God.

7. *Divine immutability*. The immutability, or changelessness,

of God is entailed by his eternity (in the sense of timelessness). St Augustine stated the truth of this immutability in Platonic terms. St Thomas restated it in terms of Aristotle's contrast between potentiality and act. God, being self-existent, is pure act; he actualises all his potentialities simultaneously; hence there is no form or degree of being that he can either acquire or lose. These metaphysical statements correspond to the moral changelessness which the Hebrews attributed to Yahweh, and which they expressed through the ideas of 'faithfulness', 'truth' and 'steadfast love' (which is the R.S.V.'s translation of *hesed*). Malachi summed it up when he wrote: 'I am God, I change not' (16).

Two points must be noted. First, the concept of immutability does not entail the concept of predestination. The affirmation that God's will cannot change does not entail the affirmation that he imposes a changeless destiny or plan upon his human creatures. God's immutability in relation to us means that his will is set changelessly on our good. But if our good includes our freedom he must take account of this freedom in all his dealings with us. Secondly, God's immutability does not conflict with petitionary prayer; for the true aim of such prayer is not to change God's will but to ask for such things as are in accordance with it.

God, then, co-operates with our free decisions and performs some of his actions in answer to our prayers. Yet in so doing he does not in the least attenuate his immutability; for he co-operates with, and responds to, us in ways that are determined by his changeless wisdom and power. Although he adapts himself to our circumstances he is not in the least changed by them. Indeed, the very fact that he continuously adapts himself to us is a sign of his changeless love.

8. *Divine impassibility.* Impassibility can be given a meaning that is nothing more than an amplification of immutability. It can mean that God is incapable of suffering change from either an external or an internal cause. But the word means particularly that he cannot experience sorrow, sadness or pain. That God is impassible in this sense was an axiom of Platonic theology. It was also considered to be

axiomatic by the Christian Fathers and the medieval schoolmen. Although it has been challenged by many twentieth-century theists it has not lacked defenders (notably Von Hügel in the second volume of his 'Essays and Addresses').

This is the most questionable aspect of classical theism. It is exposed to the following objections. First, how can God be Love and not be pained (as human love at its best is pained) by evil? Certainly God's love infinitely exceeds ours. Yet can we speak at all meaningfully of it if there is no correspondence between it and human love at this crucial point? Secondly, there is the fact of the Incarnation. Admittedly (according to the orthodox formulation of it) the divine and human natures of Jesus were distinct. Yet they were centred in one 'person' and united by a perfect interchange of properties (*communicatio idiomatum*). To put it simply, it is very hard to believe that if God fully became Man he did not experience any of the pains that his Manhood endured. Lastly, von Hügel admits that if God is Love we must speak of him as One who 'sympathises' with us. But can one meaningfully speak of a real sympathy from which all sorrow and pain are absent?

However, can the postulation of suffering in God be made compatible with belief in his immutability? I suggest that it can be so if we remember the following facts.

(a) The sorrow and pain that God experiences are wholly vicarious; they consist entirely in his imaginative response to the sin and suffering that afflict his creatures. Nothing in his own nature can cause him either physical or mental pain. He cannot know physical pain; for he is incorporeal. Also he cannot know mental pain. He cannot know the pain of guilt (for he is pure goodness); he cannot know the pain of loneliness (for he is wholly self-sufficient in his triune life); he cannot know the pain of fear (for he is the omniscient ruler of all things).

(b) Therefore, any suffering that God endures through his love for his creatures is immediately transfigured by the joy that is necessarily his within his uncreated Godhead. We cannot, of course, conceive (much less imagine) this trans-

24

figuration. Yet we can reasonably postulate it if we recollect that God *is* joy (as — to anticipate my next section — he *is* all his attributes); that creatures, by their very nature, cannot modify the being of the omnipotent Creator; and that God, through his omniscience and omnipotence, knows and wills the ultimate victory of good over evil (17).

(c) There are analogies even in human experience to the transfiguration of God's sorrow in his joy. Thus a priest can rejoice in his efforts to bring salvation to sinners (even while he loathes the sin). Again, a doctor can rejoice in his task of healing the sick (even while he loathes disease). In each case the joy is constituted by an inner, self-diffusing goodness. In each case, too, the joy assimilates and transforms the evil. Even in the most difficult case finite spirituality, at its best, thus points to the infinite spirituality of God.

Obviously much more could be said on both sides than I have either the space or the competence to say. I can only add one thing. Any fruitful approach to the question requires a special effort at maintaining both the necessary scope and the necessary limits of intellectual understanding. We must be able to see that our viewpoint is reasonable — that it is compatible with every extension of our speculative powers. Yet we cannot hope to give it 'cash-value' in terms of our own experience; for if God's inner life is (in the last resort) a mystery, the relation of his life to our finite lives must be doubly so.

9. *Divine simplicity*. If God is infinite he must be simple; he must express his whole nature in a single act; for if any part of his nature were not expressed he would be *pro tanto* limited. Alternatively, if there were any property that he did not express he would not be self-existent; for a self-existent being — a being in whom essence and existence are identical — must express his whole nature simultaneously.

The point can be amplified through the Aristotelian categories of potentiality and act. If God is infinite or self-existent there cannot be any potentialities in his being that are not actualised; he must exist as pure, unconditioned Act. Consequently, there must be a perfect coincidence of all his

25

attributes. Thus his intelligence must coincide perfectly with his will, and his justice with his love.

Aquinas states God's simplicity thus:

> Since there is no composition of quantitative parts in God, for he is not a body; nor a composition of matter and form; nor are his nature and complete substantiality distinct; nor his essence and existence; nor is there a composition of genus and difference; nor of subject and accidents — it is plain that God is altogether simple and nowise composite (18).

All God's attributes therefore coexist in a perfect unity:

> The plurality of names for divine perfections does not militate against divine simplicity. Perfections which are diversified in other things by different forms exist in God by identical virtue. An analogy may be drawn from the faculties of knowing. The single ability of mind knows all things which the sensibility knows by diverse abilities — and many other things besides. Every kind of perfection, which other things obtain only in varied diversity, is possessed by God in his own single and simple being — yea and many more (19).

God's simplicity wholly surpasses our understanding. When we apply the word 'simple' to created entities we normally mean that they are lower in the scale of being than more complex entities. 'Simple' (from our finite standpoint) means 'less rich in being', and so 'farther removed from the infinite richness of the Creator', than 'complex'. Thus an atom is simple compared with a molecule, a one-bar melody compared with a symphony, a child compared with a man. Hence 'simple' can be used in a tone of disparagement, as when we say of an adult that he is 'simple-minded' or 'a simpleton'. In so saying we mean that he lacks the complexity, the many-sidedness, which he ought to possess as a fully grown member of his species.

Admittedly, we can also use 'simple' and its cognates as

26

terms of commendation with reference to internally complex entities. Thus we can praise a writer for making a complicated subject simple because, while avoiding over-simplification, he expounds his subject with the maximum degree of clarity and economy. Similarly, we can praise a highly intelligent and many-sided person for possessing a 'simple' character. In attributing simplicity to him we mean that he is free from hypocrisy or guile, that he is direct in his emotional responses and his speech, and that all his attitudes are integrated or (as we sometimes put it) 'of a piece'.

Yet although these examples point towards – and are indeed created images of – God's simplicity, they are not parallel to it. In each case the division into parts remains. The writer's success consists in his capacity to interrelate the various parts of his subject lucidly. The simplicity we admire in my hypothetical person's character consists in the integration of elements that are by nature disparate and that can never achieve a perfect degree of coinherence. All anyone can hope for (even with the aid of divine grace) is that his personality will achieve increasing degrees of integration. An absolute degree – a perfect identification of one mental act with every other – can be achieved only by God; for only he is without the division into parts imposed by spatial and temporal limitations, only he is free from external conditions, and (above all) only he possesses a complete identity of essence and existence (so that he is all that he could become).

Yet one point remains to be stressed. To affirm that all God's properties are identical is not to affirm that they merge into an undifferentiated unity. God is really intelligence and really will; he is really love and really justice. The doctrine of God's simplicity does not deny the real distinctiveness of his attributes. It affirms that the distinctiveness of each attribute so perfectly interpenetrates the distinctiveness of all the other attributes that each attribute fully expresses everything that the others express.

In order to combine the affirmation of God's simplicity with the affirmation of his attributes' objective reality, theologians and religious writers apply attributes to God in a

27

self-existent form. Thus they speak of God as One who *is* Intelligence, Will, Love and so on. Consequently it is natural for the theist to address God in prayer by one of these names. Yet even this mode of description does not enable us to comprehend God's essence; for we cannot grasp the manner in which these self-existent attributes coinhere.

10. *Divine perfection*. God is obviously perfect in being if he is infinite; and if he is perfect in being he must be perfect in every attribute that self-existent being can possess. Conversely if he were defective in any spiritual attribute he would be defective in being, and so he would not be self-existent. As Aquinas puts it, 'although being an existent thing does not involve being living or wise (for nothing partaking of existence need partake every mode of existence), nevertheless, existence itself does involve life and wisdom (for subsistent existence itself cannot lack any perfection of existence') (20).

This argument demonstrates, not only God's intellectual attributes, but also his moral goodness. 'Perfection' here must include moral perfection; for if God were morally imperfect in his nature he would be to that extent defective in his being. This moral extension of the argument admittedly rests on the premiss that good, not evil, is the fulfilment of spiritual being. If anyone chose to say that fulfilment of such being consists in evil he could not be logically refuted. But the theist is surely permitted to exclude consideration of sheer diabolism when he is constructing his metaphysical premisses.

Doubtless people do not normally believe in God's goodness by means of this speculative deduction from his self-existence. They believe in it (as they believe in his existence) by a spiritual intuition and the various forms of religious experience that this intuition engenders. Thus, although Plato's ideal philosopher approaches the Form of the Good by dialectic, he finally apprehends it by immediate insight. Most theists who belong to the Judaeo-Christian tradition apprehend God's goodness through the claims of conscience. Their awareness of the categorical imperative exerted by the

28

moral law (and by the moral values to which this law is related) testifies to the reality of a holy Lawgiver. This testimony is supernaturally fulfilled in Christ as the Incarnation of God and therefore the perfect revelation of his will.

There is, however, a major objection to the idea of God's absolute perfection. It may be said that some divine 'perfections' are mutually incompatible. This possibility was envisaged by Leibniz when he said that the ontological argument rested on the assumption that the idea of an absolutely perfect being is self-consistent. Theists claim that the idea is self-consistent, and that any clash between God's attributes is apparent, not real. I shall illustrate this claim through the example that is most frequently discussed. It has often been asserted that God cannot be both infinitely just and infinitely merciful. But (so the theist would claim) this incompatibility is not real; it results from a partial, anthropomorphic view of God's nature. Let us agree that God, being pure Love, is always merciful; his mercy 'endures for ever'. Let us further agree that God's justice means primarily (in so far as it is predicable of his own uncreated being) his absolute righteousness or holiness. The great insight of St Paul in his doctrine of justification was twofold. First, God's righteousness (as revealed in Christ) consists in his desire (prompted by love) to restore his sinful creatures to a right relation with himself. Secondly, the only manner in which God could thus restore fallen mankind was by the sacrificial mercy of the Cross. Such a view of divine justice does not exclude the ideas of 'penalty' and 'retribution' which are involved in our human idea of justice; but it reduces them to a secondary status. All sinners bear the penalty of their sins in the form of an inevitable alienation from God. And there is at least the possibility that they will be excluded from his presence for ever. Yet if this exclusion occurs (or will occur) it will not be because God has decided for retribution and against mercy; it will be because the sinner has, of his own free will, rejected a mercy that is infinite and ever-present.

Obviously, the preceding paragraph needs to be amplified; but such an amplification is the task of Biblical and dogmatic theology. At least I hope I have said enough to show that the

29

theist can make out a plausible case for the coinherence in an infinite form of spiritual attributes that may at first sight seem opposed. This case is not a merely speculative one; it is grounded in the original interpretation of the Christian Gospel.

11. *Divine omniscience*. This means that God knows all things. One of the most obvious signs of our finiteness is our ignorance. There are innumerable things that no human mind can know, or that even the most penetrating human mind can know only in an imperfect manner. But God knows all things perfectly. The perfection of his knowledge is shown both in its manner and in its extent.

So far as the manner of God's knowledge is concerned, it excels human knowledge in being wholly intuitive. Our knowledge, although it contains intuitive elements, is largely discursive. It is acquired and confirmed by comparing, classifying, abstracting and drawing inferences from sense-data. God has no need of these piecemeal processes; he knows all things by a direct intellectual intuition; his knowledge (as Aquinas expresses it) 'is not reasoned or discursive, though he knows all reasonings and processes' (21).

Correlatively, God's knowledge differs from human knowledge in extent. Because we must build up our knowledge discursively and within a limited setting we can never know anything completely; and there are many things which we cannot know at all. For the same reasons our knowledge is fallible. We sometimes think we are in possession of the truth when we are really in error. God, however, knows all things perfectly and infallibly through his absolute mode of intellectual intuition.

This double perfection of God's knowledge can be deduced not only from his self-existence, but also from the fact that he is the Creator. Because he creates all things *ex nihilo* he must know all things intuitively and completely. Indeed, in knowing himself he must (as Aquinas affirms) know also the nature of everything that does or can exist; for there is nothing in the world that does not pre-exist as an idea in his mind and that does not owe its being to his will.

The world is merely the projection into actuality of the possibilities that his mind contains.

Two main problems arise here. First, does God know the world as a succession of events, or does he know it as a single, timeless present? Theists who follow Aquinas adopt the second of these alternatives. In the eyes of God, they say, events that happened in 200 B.C. are as much present as my existence now in 1970. The argument in favour of this view is this. If God is eternal, and if all his acts express his essence, his consciousness must be in all respects eternal; but if he knew the world in its temporal form his consciousness (and so his being) would be temporally conditioned.

However, there are two objections to the view that God knows temporal events timelessly. First, if time is real how can it be known timelessly? It is easy to understand that God, in knowing himself, knows timelessly all the possibilities that the world actualises; but he does not thus know them *as actual*; and if their actuality is objectively temporal I find it very hard to see how we can meaningfully speak of them as being timelessly known.

Secondly, even if it is possible for God to know temporal events timelessly he could not thus know them, if they are really temporal, as they really are. And if he does not know them in all respects as they really are his knowledge of them is incomplete. It could even be plausibly maintained that God would be in error if he thought that a really temporal world was timeless because it appeared timeless to him.

Admittedly the latter objection loses some of its force if time is illusory or if it only has the 'phenomenal' objectivity accorded to it by Kant. Yet even if time is illusory, or only phenomenally objective, it unquestionably seems real to us. The assumption of this reality governs our whole existence. Surely, then, God must reckon with — must, indeed, have some positive understanding of — this assumption, even if the assumption is erroneous; for without such understanding he would not have a complete knowledge of human mentality (22).

In answer to the objection that if God knew the world successively he would be temporally conditioned, three

31

things can, I think, be said. First, we are aware of many things that are alien to, and that do not in the least change, our nature. The mind does not *substantially* become what it knows. Secondly (and in particular), we do not become the past and the future when we contemplate them in the present. On the contrary, the very act of such contemplation shows a limited transcendence of the time-process. Thirdly, Aquinas insists that God knows things in their actual singularity, although he himself is non-individuated. Similarly, God knows evil although he himself is pure Goodness. Why, then, should we not allow that, although he himself is timeless, he can know temporal events successively?

Moreover, the view that God knows temporal events successively does not conflict with the view that he knows them intuitively. We could still hold that he takes in each stage of the process at a single glance. Both the mode, and consequently the extent, of God's knowledge would still differ in kind from its human copies.

The second problem concerns human acts of free will. There is no difficulty in supposing that God knows these if his knowledge of them is timeless, as Aquinas points out:

> At the height of eternity God regards all things from above the movement of time. Events that come to be in time are already present to him. When I see Socrates sitting down, my knowledge is certain and infallible, but it imposes no necessity on Socrates to sit. And so God, in looking at things which to us are past, present, or future, infallibly and certainly knows them as present realities, yet without imposing on them the necessity of existing (23).

However, if God's knowledge of the world is successive he could not foreknow future freely chosen acts (if we interpret freedom in the indeterminist's sense, according to which a free act is one of which we can without qualification say that the agent could have chosen otherwise); for God could 'know' (in contrast with 'guess') such acts only if they were predictable; but if they were predictable they would not be free. Yet the absence of such knowledge on God's part would not imperil his omniscience; for he can know only such things as are knowable. Furthermore, God would still know, immediately and completely, both every possibility of choice and every possible consequence of it.

I must stress that I have done no more than outline two interpretations of 'omniscience', and that a rationally justified choice between them presupposes a more extensive analysis than the one I have been able to offer (24). However, on both interpretations the distinctive meaning of 'omniscience' (as this is entailed by 'infinity') is preserved.

12. *Omnipotence*. To call God 'omnipotent' can mean either (a) that he is ruler over all things, or (b) that he can do all things. Both meanings are entailed by the idea of his infinity.

(a) Obviously, if God is the infinite Creator he rules over all finite things he has created. The ways in which he rules — the forms of his providence and grace — fall outside the scope of this book.

(b) This is the sense that is normally given to 'omnipotence'. This sense, too, is required by the affirmation of infinity. If God is infinite he must be able to do all things *which are in accordance with his nature*. The last seven words are crucial. God cannot do what is logically impossible (and so what is contrary to reason); he cannot make $4 + 2 = 7$. He cannot change the principles of morality; he cannot make charity wrong or cheating right. He cannot violate human freedom, which is a spiritual good that he himself has given.

No one is likely to dispute these formal definitions. The notorious difficulty occurs when we attempt to square God's omnipotence with his love. If God is both infinitely loving and omnipotent why does he permit evil? A full consideration of this question belongs to another volume in this series. Here I must be content with a few observations.

The answer given by classical theism to this question consists in stressing the last of the qualifications which I introduced into the idea of omnipotence. God has given man freedom; moral evil (or sin) results from man's abuse of this gift; hence both God's omnipotence and his love are secured.

33

But this answer is inadequate for several reasons. In the first place, it is an obvious fact (which the Christian doctrine of Original Sin supports) that each person is born with evil inclinations for which he is not responsible. Again, the existence of these inclinations cannot be convincingly explained (as traditional theology has sought to explain it) as the effect of Adam's 'fall'; for evolutionary biology makes it impossible for us to posit such a first man and his pristine innocence, and in any case it is extremely hard to see how anyone without evil tendencies could, in full knowledge, rebel against the will of his loving Creator. Finally the Adam story cannot explain 'natural' evils —earthquakes, famine, drought, disease.

I, therefore, conclude that we cannot reconcile evil with God's omnipotence by recourse to the idea of free will. Nor can we evade the problem by declaring evil to be an 'illusion'; for theists hold that evil is fully real (25), and Christian theism in particular presupposes this reality in its proclamation of Christ as the Victor and Redeemer.

Can we, then, rationally square the existence of evil with belief in an omnipotent God of love? I believe that we can do so if, and only if, we can show (a) that the emergence of moral evil (or sin) was virtually inevitable in the world that God has created, (b) that evil can become the means for obtaining a good which could not be obtained by any other means, and (c) that God himself has done all that is congruous with his nature to overcome evil by good. I can here only state my belief that these conditions are fulfilled in the ways described by John Hick in his 'Evil and the God of Love' (26).

(c) Classical theism (3)

Four further elements in classical theism need to be examined — the ideas of divine transcendence, divine immanence, divine personality, and the attribution of the terms 'objective' and 'subjective' to God.

First, the God of classical theism is *transcendent*. This

34

adjective means (a) that God is substantially distinct from the world, (b) that he does not need the world, and (c) that he is incomprehensible.

(a) God is substantially distinct from the world. Conversely the world is not in any sense a part of God. We can certainly say that God's act in creating the world is the expression of his nature; we can even say that the world itself is such an expression, if by this we mean that it is a created likeness of his perfection; but we cannot say that the world expresses his nature if by this we mean that it actually shares in his self-existent being.

Admittedly some theologians have spoken of man's final destiny in terms of 'divinisation'. In so doing they follow 2 Peter 1:4, where it is said that Christians are meant to become 'partakers of the divine nature'. But this language must be interpreted in the context of faith in the Incarnation. Christians do not share in the divine nature immediately; for this would be impossible even with the aid of grace; they share in it only in so far as it is mediated, by the Spirit, through the humanity assumed by the divine Son.

Again, some Christian and Muslim mystics have spoken as if at the moment of spiritual union they have become actually identical with, or absorbed into, the Godhead. Yet even those who have so spoken have sometimes subsequently qualified their words — words which are in any case attempts to communicate the incommunicable. All that need be noted here is that however close a theistic mystic may be, and feel, to God through his life of prayer and love, he (or she) remains substantially distinct from God as the Creator.

A word must be said concerning the spatial imagery of 'height' with which 'transcendence' is associated. This imagery, which occurs copiously in theistic literature, is inevitable; for the mind is bound to use images in order to give positive, concrete content to the Transcendent. But it is of the utmost importance that we regard all images as means towards an end to which they are always inadequate. Since God is incorporeal he must be unimageable; so that we must constantly negate all images in seeking to know him.

(b) God's transcendence means that he has no need of the

world. Because he is self-sufficient within his triune life of love he cannot require anything for the fulfilment of his being, or, therefore, for his beatitude. If we ask why, then, God creates the world we can only say that he does so because the very nature of his goodness (being identical with his love) is to diffuse itself in a sheerly altruistic form of creativity. Such altruism is bound to surpass our understanding. And so I approach the third element in the idea of transcendence.

(c) God's transcendence means that he is incomprehensible. Even if his nature merely differed from all other natures to a superlative degree we could not conceive it fully; but since his nature (being infinite and self-existent) differs in kind from all other natures we cannot conceive it at all. Although we can apprehend God we cannot comprehend him.

God's incomprehensibility is affirmed throughout the Judaeo-Christian tradition. Thus in the Second Isaiah we read: 'For my thoughts are not your thoughts, neither are your ways my ways, says the Lord' (27). Similarly, Aquinas writes that 'though in himself supremely knowable, God surpasses the power of a limited intelligence by very excess of truth' (28), and that 'to realize that God is far beyond anything we think, that is the mind's achievement' (29). This is also a constant theme among the mystics. Thus 'The Cloud of Unknowing' affirms of God: 'By love may he be gotten and holden, but by thought never.'

God's incomprehensibility has been stated in three main ways during the last two hundred years.

First, Kant affirmed, on the basis of his critical principles, that although the human mind can postulate God's existence as a regulative Idea, it cannot know him either by means of the categories through which we understand finite objects or by a non-sensuous intuition. Although many theists would dispute Kant's claim that we cannot have *any* knowledge of God by these means they must agree with him that our mental categories do not enable us to give a positive and direct description of God's essence.

Secondly, there is the theology of Kierkegaard and those

36

(especially Barth and Bultmann) who are indebted to him. In deliberate contrast with Hegel's monism (according to which the human intellect can adequately know the Absolute), Kierkegaard insisted that God, as the infinite and eternal Creator, is wholly unknowable. Barth's theology is similarly founded on belief in the 'qualitative difference' between God and man. Combining this belief with a Calvinist view of Original Sin, Barth holds that we can know God only by faith in Christ as his self-revelation. Like Kierkegaard, Barth holds that all our speech concerning God is 'dialectical'. We are compelled to make paradoxical, seemingly contradictory statements concerning God without being able to synthesise them in a unitary vision.

There can be no doubt that Kierkegaard, Barth and Bultmann have rendered a major service to Christian theism in emphasising (against Hegelianism) God's transcendence and consequent incomprehensibility. Yet it is doubtful whether they justify even the limited theistic assertions which they make from the standpoint of faith. I shall return to this point shortly.

Lastly, the concept of transcendence has been expressed through the concept of 'mystery'. The latter concept is, of course, an old one; but it has been given two new and important interpretations in this century. The first of these is the one expounded by Otto in his 'The Idea of the Holy'. Religion, he maintained, consists in the sense of a *mysterium tremendum* – a reality that transcends our understanding and that on account of this transcendence induces awe in those who experience it. The second interpretation is derived from Marcel's contrast between 'problems' and 'mysteries'. In ordinary life and scientific investigation we are often confronted with problems which we feel compelled to solve through the relevant processes of reason. But we also encounter mysteries – that is, forms of being (especially other personalities) that cannot be fully understood, and towards which the appropriate attitude is one of contemplation. God, on this view, is the supreme mystery – the Presence who is wholly incomprehensible and who must be approached with the maximum degree of loving contemplation (30).

However, we here face a notorious difficulty. On the one hand theists assert that God is incomprehensible. On the other hand they make positive affirmations concerning his character. Some theologians, following Kierkegaard, have left this antinomy as it stands. But surely some attempt to solve it must be made if theism is not to be irrational at its very core. There are three possible solutions.

1. It may be said that our positive symbols of God cannot be given an objective reference; they are purely subjective constructions; they signify merely our response to a totally non-characterisable Godhead. But this 'solution' is invalidated by two simple observations. First, how can we validly worship and obey God unless we have grounds for believing that the theistic language of worship and obedience is objectively true? Secondly, this solution departs completely from the Bible and the main forms of philosophical theism.

2. It may be said that although there is a correspondence between finite symbols and their divine object we cannot specify this correspondence or give any reasons for postulating it. But this solution is even less satisfactory than the first. It is not only exposed to the two objections that I brought against the first; it is also self-contradictory in both claiming that symbols refer to God and expressing agnosticism concerning the manner in which they do so.

3. We must therefore postulate a real analogy between finite symbols and their divine object if we are to validate their use. There are two relevant types of analogy — an analogy of being (*analogia entis*), and an analogy of grace or faith (*analogia gratiae* or *fidei*). The first type is distinctive of Catholic, and the second of Protestant, thought.

According to the analogy of being there is both a likeness and an unlikeness between God and man. They are like in so far as both exist *per se* and both exhibit those forms of spirituality that distinguish man from sub-human creatures. But God differs in kind from man in so far as only he exists *a se*, so that only he expresses spirituality in an infinite form.

Aquinas maintains that on account of this analogy of being between creatures and the Creator we can speak of him

38

through terms drawn from the created order by an 'analogy of proportionality'. We can validly assert that just as wisdom, goodness and power inhere in men in a form appropriate to their finite being, so they inhere in God in a manner appropriate to his self-existence. Admittedly we do not know *how* they inhere in God; for we have no positive notion of self-existence. Yet we can affirm *that* they inhere in him self-sufficiently.

Barth rejects the whole idea of *analogia entis*. In his view there is no similarity between the creature and the Creator; so that we cannot take terms from our descriptions of created being and apply them by analogy to the Creator. We must rely solely on an analogy of grace (*analogia gratiae*). 'It is', to quote from John Macquarrie's summary, 'God's grace in his revelation that establishes a community between himself and man, so that we can speak of him in human words. Not an analogy of being but an analogy of grace makes our talk of God veracious. This view of analogy preserves both the divine initiative and the entire passivity of the human mind in our knowledge of God' (31).

It is clear that positive language referring to a transcendent God can be justified only by the doctrine of analogy in one of these two forms. It seems to me that the second form (if it is taken, as Barth takes it, to be self-sufficient) is exposed to fatal objections, of which I shall mention only two. First, how can God reveal himself as Man unless there is an analogy of being between him and his human creatures? Secondly, the very idea of a personal God who reveals himself by grace requires justification.

Hence theists are forced to rely on the first form of analogy — the analogy of being and the consequent analogy of proportionality. They must assume that there is a likeness, as well as an unlikeness, between God and his creatures, and that the likeness entitles us to attribute spiritual properties to God in a manner appropriate to his self-existence (even though our positive knowledge of these properties is restricted to their finite modes).

Although I cannot fully justify this assumption here I shall mention four points relevant to its justification.

(a) The ascription of spiritual properties to God is not totally separate from, or independent of, the affirmation of his transcendence. On the contrary (as I have tried to show in the previous two sections), 'transcendence' for the theist means, precisely, 'self-existence'. And (as I also tried to show) once we grasp the idea of self-existence we can see that it entails the idea of spiritual perfection.

(b) There is bound to be some degree of likeness between the creature and the Creator. If God is self-existent and if he brings the world into being *ex nihilo* he must, if he creates at all, create beings that to some degree resemble him. If he *is* existence, and if, therefore, there is no pre-existent being to which he must conform his will, his creatures must in some way reflect his nature. According to theism there cannot be any form of existence except either God's own self-existence or some finite copy of it.

(c) When we reflect we can see that the very idea of creation implies a personal Creator; for only a spiritual act of will can bring the world into being *ex nihilo*. This reflection becomes even more pointed when we consider that the only conceivable motive for God's act of creation is one of love. We thus cannot even begin to speak meaningfully of 'creation' without implying the analogy of a personal Creator.

(d) This analysis of 'creation' is confirmed by the Scriptural affirmation that God created man 'in his own image'. *Pace* Barth, the concept of *analogia entis*, so far from being alien to Biblical revelation, is an essential part of it.

Let us next consider the complementary fact of God's *immanence*. This fact is implied in the theistic concept of creation. Theism differs from deism in its assertion that God's creative activity is continuous. Every creature at every moment depends on his immediate power for its existence. Aquinas expresses this truth thus:

> Since the infinite must be everywhere and in all things, we have now to consider whether this applies also to God. God is in all things, not, indeed, as part of their essence, or

40

as a quality, but in the manner that an efficient cause is present to that on which it acts. An efficient cause must be in touch with the product of its action immediately, and this by its own power. Now since God's very essence is his existence, created existence is his proper effect. This effect God causes, not only when things first begin to be, but so long as they continue to be. While a thing endures, therefore, God must be present to it according to its mode of being. Existence is most intimate to each and deepest in all reality since it is the heart of all perfection. Hence, God is in all things, and intimately (32).

We must note Aquinas's statement that 'God is in all things, not, indeed, as part of their essence, or as a quality, but in the manner that an efficient cause is present to that on which it acts.' God does not impart his own uncreated life to creatures. On the contrary his immanence consists precisely in their continuous dependence on his creative power.

This power, moreover, is spiritual and invisible. It is wholly hidden from our sight. We can perceive and understand finite causes by observation, correlation and (where appropriate) introspection. But we cannot thus detect or (even partially) comprehend God's immanence. God, as the primary cause of all things, remains perpetually concealed within them and their secondary causes.

God's immanence, therefore, like his transcendence, is a mystery. Although we have rational grounds for postulating it, we cannot make it comprehensible. Indeed the very word itself can be misleading. 'Immanence' can easily suggest that God 'dwells in' or 'fills' the world (and especially human souls) as a man may be said to dwell in his house, or water to fill a jar. Yet God does not impart any of his substance to creatures; and in any case the mode of his immanence is entirely non-spatial. It may therefore be better to speak of God's presence 'to' the creature; but this is not wholly satisfactory, for it could be taken to imply that the creature exists independently of God's creative act; and in any case the modality of the act remains unknowable.

Admittedly the Biblical writers speak of God or God's

41

Spirit, as 'filling' both physical nature and human persons. But we must remember that these writers spoke in an imaginative rather than a conceptual way, and that they did not submit their statements to metaphysical criticism. From the immediate standpoint of religious experience, and in terms of the thought-forms that were available to them, their language was justified. However, all finite terms, and especially those with corporeal associations, must be qualified when they are applied to the infinite and incorporeal God.

Next let us examine the idea of God's *personality*. If God possesses the spiritual attributes I have mentioned he must be personal; for these are the marks that distinguish personal from sub-personal forms of being. If, then, the analogies of being and proportionality are valid we can speak of God as one who expresses in an infinite form those personal characteristics that we express finitely. As pure Spirit he is the archetype of personality.

There are three possible substitutes for a straightforward ascription of personality to God. All of them involve grave difficulties.

(a) It may be said that God is really supra-personal, and that personal symbols of him are merely finite attempts to express the inexpressible; they are only modes in which a wholly supra-personal reality appears to untutored minds. This view (which was explicitly held in the East by the Indian philosopher Sankara, and in the West by F. H. Bradley) cannot withstand two (among other) criticisms. First, the idea of a non-personal form of being that is not sub-personal is meaningless; for it is one to which we cannot give any content. Secondly, the idea can have no place in Christian theism, which rests on the conviction that the God to whom reason, experience and revelation point is an infinite Spirit who, as such, is infinitely personal.

The next two interpretations are attempts to mediate between a supra-personal and a fully personal view of God.

(b) It is sometimes said that while God has personal properties he also has, or may have, other properties that are

42

supra-personal. However, there are three objections to this view. First (as I have already said) the idea of such a supra-personal view of God is meaningless. Secondly, we cannot posit different levels or grades in God if his essence and existence are identical. Thirdly, this view has no support from the Bible, which everywhere presupposes that God is ultimately — in his inmost being — personal. This presupposition is shown with special clarity in Christ's use of the symbol 'Father'.

(c) It may be said that it is sufficient to affirm that God is personal in his relation to his creatures. But it is manifestly insufficient. If God can relate himself personally to men there must be some element in his nature that is intrinsically personal. And so we are forced to choose between (b) and an unqualified form of personal theism.

If, then, we assent to classical theism we must affirm that God is ultimately, fully and intrinsically personal. Of course the validity of this affirmation depends on the validity of analogical predication and of the *analogia entis* on which the latter rests. I cannot here attempt to establish this validity beyond reminding the reader of the four bases of validation I suggested.

There is, however, one point on which I must touch. It may be said that 'personality' is a more limited term than 'spirituality' in two ways. First, each human person is constituted by a union between his soul and his body; and his body is, if not a necessary, at least a contingent, sign of his personal identity. Secondly, we cannot divorce the idea of 'personality' from the idea of 'individuality'; but each person (to use the metaphysical terminology on which classical theism rests) is individuated by being a particular, unique member of a species which, in turn, is a subdivision of a genus. However, God is incorporeal and (as Aquinas explicitly stated) is not a member of a genus.

I have already given a general answer to the first question in speaking of God's incorporeality. If we admit that mind is ontologically distinct from matter we have no right to deny the possibility that even in the case of man mental activities (and the spiritual subject-self in which they inhere) can

43

survive in an incorporeal form. Consequently we have no right to deny that they can exist in God in an infinite form.

The question of individuality can be answered simply by observing that we are not logically obliged to restrict 'individual' to membership of a class. There may be a being whose individuality consists in the fact that he stands outside all finite classes as the Infinite who transcends them all. Theists claim that there actually is such a being, and that he is therefore individuality, or personal distinctness, *par excellence*. As Gilson puts it, 'his existential purity individuates God and sets him apart from all the rest' (33).

There is one more matter that requires clarification. In recent years, largely owing to the influence of existentialism, it has been debated whether faith is 'objective' or 'subjective'. Here, as elsewhere, it is necessary to distinguish between the order of being and the order of knowing. In this book I am concerned primarily with the former, but I cannot avoid discussion of the latter. Ontology cannot be finally separated from epistemology.

So far as my ontological purpose is concerned, the interpretation of 'objective' and 'subjective' is clear. God is objective in the sense that he is an independently existing reality. But he is also subjective in the sense that he is the subject of personal experience – an 'I' who can be addressed as 'Thou' in prayer.

On the epistemological plane also, theism is both objective and subjective. It is objective in so far as theists claim to know God both by a direct apprehension and by descriptive statements (within the limits imposed by the analogy of proportionality). It is subjective in so far as this apprehension of God is unlikely to occur, and certainly cannot develop, without the personal attitudes of wonder, humility and contemplation. The knowledge of God is also subjective in so far as the only positive meaning we can give to our theistic language is the one which it has in our own finite experience.

This is the best point at which to comment on the account which existentialists give of God. Kierkegaard and his theistic successors deserve our gratitude for their emphasis on God's

44

transcendence, personality, and the consequently personal nature of our relation to him. Yet from the standpoint of classical theism, they err by excess of zeal in the following respects (34).

1. In their commendable desire to stress the subjective (= 'personal') nature of God and his relationship to his human creatures, existentialists are apt to assume that all speculation concerning him converts him into an object (= 'thing') — an 'It' in place of an 'I'. This assumption rests on a confusion of epistemology with ontology. Because we think 'about' God we do not thereby convert him into a 'thing'. On the contrary, we often 'think about' — formulate concepts of — those human persons who are bound to us by the closest ties of affection. Our objective thought about, and our subjective response to, them continually interact in mutually enriching ways.

2. Existentialists impose an intolerable limit on theism when they restrict theistic statements to those which are immediately relevant to the believer's subjective, or personal, existence. This restriction is doubly false. First, theistic faith is basically the experience of God as a *mysterium tremendum* who merits adoration for his own sake. Secondly, theists have often been aware of God through nature without any reference to any human situation.

3. Existentialists are bound to imply that God is an objective reality and that objectively valid statements can be made concerning him. Yet they fail to justify even those statements that they make from their limited standpoint. Jaspers's concept of 'ciphers' is very obscure. And Bultmann does not offer a positive theory of theistic language (35). The more one studies the theological existentialists the more it becomes apparent that even their attenuated affirmations concerning God can be justified only by the analogy of being (and consequent analogy of proportionality) that they either reject or ignore.

4. It has become an uncriticised habit among many existentialists (and many others who have been consciously or unconsciously influenced by them) to posit an absolute contrast between the Hebraic and Greek concepts of God.

45

According to this contrast, whereas the Jews regarded God 'subjectively' as a personal and dynamic Being who acts in history, the Greeks regarded him 'objectively' as an impersonal and static Absolute that is unrelated to the world. It is then further maintained that classical theists, in using the abstract and impersonal terminology of Greek metaphysics, obscure the concrete and personalistic nature of Biblical theology.

In answer it is enough to make the following the points.

In the first place, the abstract terminology used by classical theists is not intrinsically tied to either a personal or an impersonal view of God. Thus the terms 'essence', 'existence', 'immutability', 'actuality', could refer to either an impersonal Absolute or the personal God of the Bible. Admittedly 'omniscience' and 'omnipotence' imply that the Being to which they refer possesses a mind and will; but they do not imply any particular mode in which he exercises these faculties; nor do they entail any view concerning his particular relation to mankind.

Again, Christian theists have always speculated against the background of Scriptural belief in a personal Creator and Redeemer. This is shown with special clarity in the case of Aquinas. All his most developed reflections concerning God occur in a work devoted to theology. He plainly regarded the Biblical revelation of God as both the starting-point and the goal of religious understanding. For him, no less than for St Augustine, theistic philosophy as much as theology was an activity of *fides quaerens intellectum* ('faith seeking understanding').

Lastly, and consequently, metaphysical speculation by means of abstract terminology is not, for the Christian theist, a substitute for the concrete language of the Bible. Such speculation is a 'second-order' pursuit. Its aim is to elucidate (from a philosophical point of view) the 'first-order' statements of those who originally received God's self-revelation to his people Israel.

I shall conclude this chapter with six observations that are relevant to classical theism as a whole.

46

1. Not all theists can, or need to, express their belief in the terms that I have used. These terms are, for the most part, abstract and metaphysical. Many theists are, and must be, content with much simpler language. For every spiritual and moral purpose it is enough for most believers to sum up their belief in a few words of Scripture.

2. Yet one must not draw too sharp a dividing-line between the pre-metaphysical beliefs of the non-philosophical theist and the metaphysical explication of these by theistic philosophers. Every theist is bound to give conceptual expression to his faith; for *fides* is always, to some extent, *fides quaerens intellectum*. The choice is not between a purely non-conceptual and a conceptual form of faith, but between varying degrees of conceptualisation.

3. It is reasonable to suppose that theists will continue to differ in their interpretation of the more debatable among the divine attributes. This is especially obvious in the cases of impassibility and omniscience. All theists, surely, must agree that the being of the infinite Creator cannot be changed by any creature; but they may well differ in their views on the attribution of feelings to him. Equally, they are bound to assert that the Creator knows all that can be known, but they may well differ in their assessment of what is intrinsically knowable, and of the manner in which knowable things are divinely known.

4. When such differences of interpretation arise we must often be content with an opinion that falls short of certainty; for the very fact that different interpretations are given by philosophers and theologians shows that our human understanding in these matters almost (though not quite) reaches breaking-point. Both the coexistence of certainty with doubt and the impossibility of stating an *a priori* line of demarcation between them are inevitable consequences of belief in an infinite Creator.

5. In the case of all God's attributes (and not only those that are inherently open to divergent interpretations) we must always remember the fact of God's incomprehensibility. We can never know God as he is in himself, in his uncreated essence. The most we can hope for is, on the one hand, to

indicate his mystery by limiting concepts which (in substance, if not in form) are wholly negative, and, on the other hand, to use positive analogies for which we can give a positive meaning only in terms of our own experience.

6. Philosophical theism is bound to seem barren if it is severed from its roots in religious experience. But it cannot be so severed by the truly Christian theist. The God on whom he speculates is 'the living God' whom he knows and worships as the Father of Jesus Christ.

I shall now proceed to discuss the most important non-theistic views of God — with special emphasis on those which are of relevance to my readers. In the course of this discussion, and also in my account of individual thinkers in Chapter 3, I hope to bring the preceding analysis of classical theism into fresh focus (36).

Chapter 2

(a) A finite God

Classical theism rests on the belief that God is infinite, that his infinity is to be understood primarily in terms of his self-existence, and that he is therefore the Creator of the world *ex nihilo*. But many distinguished philosophers have held that God is finite. I shall mention three — two from the ancient, and one from the modern, world.

Firstly, there is Plato. His view of a finite God is contained in his 'Timaeus'. According to the myth expounded there, God, as the supreme Craftsman, imposes on independently given matter an order that he copies from the Forms (or Ideas). His motive for doing so is that, being good and so incapable of jealousy, he wishes everything to become as like himself as possible. Plato's God is thus doubly limited — by the Forms on the one hand, and matter (or 'necessity') on the other. Christian Platonists modified Plato's views on these two crucial points by making the Forms ideas in the mind of God, and by abolishing the notion of an indeterminate 'matter' that is prior to God's creative act.

The God whom Aristotle described in his 'Metaphysics' is also finite. He is the first, unmoved, among many celestial movers; and he does not create the world which exists eternally in independence of him. He 'moves' the world by inspiring love and desire in the 'first heaven'. But he does not love the world, or even know it; he remains wholly enveloped in the purely intellectual activity of self-contemplation. Hence, although Aquinas borrowed from Aristotle's 'Metaphysics' he modified the latter by affirming that God, having created the world 'out of nothing', directs it by his providence.

In the nineteenth century belief in a finite God was strongly advocated by John Stuart Mill in his 'Theism'.

Having argued that adaptations in nature afford probability to belief in a cosmic Designer, he denied that the latter is omnipotent. God, he affirmed, does not create matter but arranges it to the extent and in the manner that its properties permit. Yet though Mill held that God is limited in power he conceded the possibility that God is limitless in intelligence.

The most sophisticated and influential formulation which the idea of a finite God has received in this century is to be found in the writings of A. N. Whitehead, who here resembles both his great Greek predecessors. Whitehead's God has both a 'primordial' and a 'consequent' nature. According to the former nature he imparts form and value to the world by ensuring the expression of eternal objects in temporal flux. According to the latter nature he incorporates the experiences of the world, and preserves its elements of good within his memory. Whitehead's God is thus limited both by the existence of the world and by the incorporation of its experiences within his being (1).

The concept of a finite God is undoubtedly attractive in many ways, of which the main ones are these.

1. A finite God, though he may be difficult to understand, is not wholly incomprehensible; he is not an absolute mystery (like the infinite Creator of classical theism). Hence he appeals to our desire for rational understanding. Conversely, the incomprehensibility of the Christian God, and the epistemological problems that it creates, are bound to constitute an offence to the speculative intellect. A finite God can be seen as the highest and integrating element in a single system of being and thought; but an infinite Creator entirely transcends all created being and all human thought about him. Hence while we can have a purely rational theology of a finite God, our reasoning concerning the God of classical theism must always terminate in a supra-rational act of faith.

2. Belief in a finite God satisfies at least some of the elements in the religious consciousness. Plato's Demiurge is moved by selfless generosity; he is sheer, self-diffusing goodness. Whitehead's God loves the world, sympathises with our sufferings, and conserves all that is worth-while in our

50

lives. Thus Whitehead describes God as 'the ideal companion who transmutes what has been lost into a living fact within his own nature' (2). Similarly, he writes of God's consequent nature that 'it is the judgment of a tenderness which loses nothing that can be saved' (3). Obviously this view of God as man's friend and the supreme power of goodness in the world meets some of the needs expressed in most religions.

3. Both Plato's Demiurge and Whitehead's God constitute answers to the questions raised by the teleological argument. Above all they help to answer the basic question why a contingent universe should be ordered rather than chaotic. Yet whether we can rationally be content with an Orderer who is not also a Creator seems to me very doubtful (on grounds that I shall state later).

4. It is at first sight easier to reconcile the existence of a finite God than it is to reconcile the existence of an infinite one with the fact of evil — especially physical, or non-moral, evil. Innocent suffering caused by purely physical means (such as earthquakes and disease for which no man is responsible) is notoriously the chief obstacle to belief in an infinite God of love. But if God's love is limited by some kind of pre-existent matter the problem seems to be soluble. As Cleanthes put it in part XI of Hume's 'Dialogues', 'supposing the Author of Nature to be finitely perfect, though far exceeding mankind; a satisfactory account may then be given of natural and moral evil, and every untoward phenomenon be explained and adjusted'.

It is on this ground that Whitehead rejects classical theism in the last paragraph of the chapter on 'God' in his 'Science and the Modern World':

Among medieval and modern philosophers, anxious to establish the religious significance of God, an unfortunate habit has prevailed of paying to Him metaphysical compliments. He has been conceived as the foundation of the metaphysical situation with its ultimate activity. If this conception be adhered to, there can be no alternative except to discern in Him the origin of all evil as well as of all good. He is then the supreme author of the play, and to

51

Him must therefore be ascribed its shortcomings as well as its success. If He be conceived as the supreme ground for limitation, it stands in His very nature to divide the Good from the Evil, and to establish Reason 'within her dominions supreme'.

5. There is perhaps some Biblical foundation for Platonic doctrine in the so-called 'P'-account of creation in Genesis 1:1-2, where we read as follows (according to the R.S.V.): 'In the beginning God created the heavens and the earth. The earth was without form and void, and darkness was upon the face of the deep; and the Spirit of God was moving over the face of the waters.' Although we cannot be certain, it seems likely that here the writer was following Babylonian cosmogony in postulating a formless chaos that preceded God's creative act.

However, the idea of a finite God is exposed to the following grave objections.

1. The idea fails to answer the cosmological question. Although it helps to explain the order that things possess, it does not explain why they exist (rather than not exist). Hence Cobb, in spite of his admiration for Whitehead's metaphysics, is obliged to abandon it at this point in order to accommodate it to a specifically Christian form of natural theology. 'God', he writes, 'must be conceived as being the reason that entities occur at all as well as determining the limits within which they can achieve their own forms' (4).

2. The being of God himself is questionable if he is finite; for just as we can ask 'What caused the world to be?', so we can ask 'What caused God to be?' It is not surprising that Whitehead wrote: 'God is the ultimate limitation, and his existence is the ultimate irrationality' (5). God's existence, in other words, is as much an inexplicable 'brute fact' as the existence of the world.

It is important to realise that Plato's Demiurge and Whitehead's God *cannot* be self-existent (and so self-explanatory); for each is limited by independently existing matter. A self-existent God must be one whose nature is identical with existence; but this identity is impossible if there are other

52

forms of existence that are not derived from him *ex nihilo*. A God who coexists with X inevitably lacks the power of being possessed by X, just as X lacks the power of being possessed by God; so that we cannot affirm that God's nature is 'to be'.

Furthermore, Whitehead's God does not merely coexist with the world; he is actually determined by it in his consequent nature through which he acquires the consciousness that his primordial nature lacks. His responsiveness to the world is the way in which he grows in perfection. Consequently Whitehead says, in summarising his theology at the close of 'Process and Reality', that it is as true to affirm that the world creates and is immanent in God as it is to say that God creates and is immanent in the world.

At both these points, then, only classical theism answers ultimate questions that the speculative reason is bound to raise. Although the idea of an infinite God does not give rational satisfaction in the sense that it permits us to comprehend his nature, it alone makes the existence of both the world and him finally intelligible. Furthermore, although an infinite God wholly transcends our understanding, the idea of him is not self-contradictory. Nor are we left without any positive knowledge of him; for since there is an 'analogy of being' between him and his creatures, we can speak of him indirectly through an 'analogy of proportionality'.

3. There are insuperable difficulties in the idea of a pre-existent matter on which God imposes form and into which he introduces value.

How do we define this matter? Is it a primitive stage in the evolutionary process? But, if so, where and on what grounds do we draw the line between matter that has and matter that has not been formed by God? It seems wholly arbitrary to say that (for example) atoms existed independently of God, and that he then formed them into molecules. Or are we to say that the whole physical and mental realms exist apart from God, who is responsible solely for introducing values into them? But this idea raises enormous problems. Values are not entirely detached from facts. On the contrary, facts of human nature are always value-laden. Thus *homo sapiens* has always been endowed with some kind of moral consciousness. Furthermore, how does the Demiurge exert his moral influence? Christians can give a tolerably reasonable account of this influence when it takes the form of a conscious response to God's 'grace'. But how could God have exerted a persuasive power over an order that has either no, or only a dim and confused, knowledge of him? Finally, it may be suggested that the matter which precedes God's creative power is a wholly indeterminate and indeterminable 'chaos', 'flux' or 'first matter' — a potentiality of being ($\mu\grave{\eta}$ $\check{o}\nu$) that is one stage removed from sheer non-being ($o\grave{\upsilon}\kappa$ $\check{o}\nu$). But this suggestion is vacuous. The idea of such a matter is totally inconceivable; it has no point of contact with our experience.

Those who postulate some form of finite being that exists independently of God's creative act cannot avoid the following antinomy. Either they regard this matter as being wholly indeterminate, so that the idea of it becomes unintelligible; or they give it a determinate character, so that they are exposed to the following criticisms. First (as I have said), any attempt to distinguish between a form of actual being that is and a form that is not theistically determined is arbitrary. Secondly, how do we explain the fact that the particular form of being that we select is adapted to divine creativity? This difficulty becomes increasingly severe as we move up the scale of finite beings. It is hard to explain how atoms (if they are regarded as 'the given') could have been so structured that they could become the basis for creating molecules; it is even harder to see how molecules (if they are regarded as 'the given') could have been so structured that they could become the basis for all those (vastly intricate) organisms that we know; it is impossible to conceive how the totality of sub-human beings (if they are regarded as 'the given') could have 'just happened' to constitute the basis for the emergence of human life and/or the mysterious 'influence' of divine goodness.

4. Does the idea of a finite God who informs pre-existent matter explain the fact of evil? It might explain non-moral (purely physical) evil if we could attribute to matter a sufficient degree of recalcitrance (or alien 'necessity', to use Plato's word). But acute difficulties are involved here. The

54

first difficulty is the one to which I have already referred. Where do we locate this recalcitrance? In molecules, in atoms, in sub-atomic matter, or some *me-ontic* substrate? Secondly, is there any empirical evidence for separating the good from the evil elements in nature, so that they can be attributed neatly to different agencies? Surely there is none whatsoever. To say that God made beneficent cells but not cancerous ones, that he arranged portions of the earth's crust that do not but not those that do erupt in earthquakes, that he directs the weather and agricultural processes when they do not but not when they do result in famine — to make divisions of this kind is to contradict the whole idea of nature's unity upon which all scientific investigation rests.

5. Although the idea of a finite God meets some religious needs it is entirely inadequate to others. In particular it cannot accommodate the two modes of religious awareness described by Schleiermacher and Otto: the feeling of absolute dependence and the sense of the numinous. Yet these modes dominate the Judaeo-Christian experience of God. They are also present in many non-Judaic forms of religion. If believers in a finite God reply to this observation that these attitudes are misplaced (in so far as they have no correlative object in an infinite Creator) the theist can reply in turn as follows.

(a) In the Judaeo-Christian tradition the attitudes are not dispensable extensions of less extreme attitudes that are compatible with the existence of a merely finite God. The experience of an absolutely creative *mysterium tremendum* has been an essential element in Judaism and Christianity from the beginning. Without it neither religion could have arisen; and without it neither could be preserved. One cannot therefore subtract this element and leave these religions intact. Once it disappears they disappear also.

(b) The doctrine of a finite God leaves no place for any form of *distinctively* religious experience. Our attitude to him differs only in degree from our attitude to a human friend for whose love, companionship and sympathy we are grateful. We can 'worship' him only in the sense that we appreciate his worth and admire it (as, to a lesser degree, we

appreciate and admire the worth of many human persons).
We can say that our worship of him is *sui generis* only if it is
permeated by a sense of him as one who is infinite in
wisdom, goodness, and power (6).

(c) Even those religious elements that are preserved by the
doctrine of a finite God are given a spiritually much more
satisfying form in theism. If a finite God can love us, how
much more is an infinite God able to do so. Moreover,
according to Christianity, God does not merely befriend us
from afar; he showed his love to the extent of becoming Man
and dying for our sake.

(d) In fact the idea of a finite God fails to validate even the
degree of comfort which it is supposed to provide. The
greatest spiritual consolation that Whitehead offers is that
God will preserve all that is of temporal value in the eternity
of his 'consequent' nature. But how can we be sure that God
himself will not perish? We cannot be sure unless he is self-
existent. This argument applies *a fortiori* to any theistically
based hope of personal immortality.

I wish to stress the limited nature of these four criticisms.
Obviously a believer in a finite God can derive inspiration
from his belief. He can also look upon such a God, and even
experience him, with modes of consciousness that must by
any normal usage be called 'religious'. My only points are
that the idea of a finite God fails to give complete assurance,
and that it excludes those experiences — especially the feeling
of absolute dependence and the response of absolute
adoration — which are alone distinctively religious and which
can be justified only on the assumption that God is the
infinite Creator.

In fact all the concepts of a finite God I have examined are
primarily philosophical, not religious. They are introduced
solely in order to complete a speculative system. Any
religious significance they have is secondary. In this they
differ from the Judaeo-Christian concept, which, though it
has metaphysical implications, is primarily the product of an
experiential response to revelation.

6. There is the question of the grounds for belief in a
finite God. The only ground I can discover — and the only

one mentioned by Cobb in his account of Whitehead — is the teleological argument. But Christian theism has additional grounds: the cosmological argument, a strong claim to have received a special revelation, and (as a response to the latter) a unique experience of God as the *mysterium tremendum et fascinans*. Moreover, the teleological argument (though I consider it to have a limited validity in many of its forms) is complicated and hard to present convincingly. Also, for the reasons I have indicated, it needs to be complemented by the cosmological argument if the demands of speculative inquiry are to be fully met.

7. The doctrine of a finite God has scarcely any basis in Judaeo-Christian revelation. The idea of a pre-existent matter that seems to be present in the opening words of Genesis is not associated anywhere else in the Bible with God's creative act. On the contrary, several theologically crucial passages of the New Testament explicitly assert that everything has been made by God (7). Moreover (as I have had more than one occasion to observe), only the belief in God's absolute creativity can justify the unconditional adoration of, and self-commitment to, him that are expressed in the Bible as a whole.

It is very important to grasp that Biblical belief in God's absolute creativity does not merely rest upon the few cosmological passages to which I have referred, but is implied by those religious attitudes that dominate the Bible. The absolute adoration of God expressed in the vision of the Apocalypse, the Pentateuchal identification of moral duty with obedience to God's will, the utter self-abandonment of the Psalmist and Jesus to God's providence, St Paul's conviction that nothing can withstand God's love — all these cannot be justified unless God is uniquely holy, imperishable and sovereign over all that exists. We cannot validly adore God in a manner inappropriate to all creatures unless he qualitatively excels them as the infinite Creator; we cannot validly identify duty with obedience to God's will unless he is self-existent goodness; we cannot validly commit ourselves without reservation to God's loving providence unless all things are completely subject to his power.

Doubtless some elements in the Bible are of temporary and accidential significance; they can be reinterpreted or 'demythologised'. But the belief in God's infinite creativity belongs to the essence of Biblical religion (and so of Biblical revelation). Without it the whole tradition of Judaism and Christianity is unintelligible.

Obviously I cannot here argue for the truth of Christian revelation. My only point is that the latter is inextricably tied to the idea of God's infinity (or self-existence). Whether a finite God is capable of revealing himself by a specific act of will (and if so in what modes) are questions I need not consider. I am concerned only to establish that the Judaeo-Christian claim to a special revelation implies the affirmation of God's infinity.

This implication is seen with unique clarity in the case of the event — the Incarnation — in which, according to Christianity, God's historical self-revelation is fulfilled. The whole point of (and indeed the 'scandal' of) the Incarnation is that it represents a union of the Infinite with the finite in one figure of history. Whether a finite God could become man is a question which, again, I need not consider. Yet even if he could do so his act in so doing would not be a parallel to the act of Incarnation in which Christians believe.

I have introduced the elements of religious experience and Christian revelation for two reasons. First, believers in a finite God sometimes assume that their belief can do justice to these elements. Secondly, the latter, to say the least, constitute an important part of the evidence that has been offered for belief in God. It would be very difficult to validate belief in God if the distinctively experiential and uniquely revelatory evidence (or, rather, putative evidence) were ruled out *ab initio*. The difficulty becomes insuperable if (as I hold) God's existence is not demonstrable by pure reason. Anyhow, according to purely rational criteria the idea of a finite God is deficient.

To sum up, the concept of a finite God — a God whose existence and activities are limited by something which he does not create — is (in spite of the undoubted attractions which I stated) subject to three basic objections. The first, the philosophical or metaphysical objection, is that we are left with the 'cosmological question' still on our hands. How did the matter on which God operates come into being? To say that it is just 'there' is to admit that there is an ultimately inexplicable element in the universe. But we cannot admit this rationally unless we can give logically conclusive objections to classical theism.

The second objection is no less strong. Although the concept of a finite God can satisfy some it cannot satisfy other elements in religion. Thus while it permits us to regard God as Friend and Helper it has no room for the theistic (and in particular the Judaeo-Christian) experience of him as a self-existent mystery on whom we are absolutely dependent and who merits our complete devotion.

Lastly, it is extremely difficult to give a satisfactory interpretation of the 'matter' on which God is supposed to impose 'form'.

(b) The God of Neo-Platonism

The non-theistic concept of God I shall now examine is due, in its fully-fledged form, to one thinker — Plotinus (205-70 A.D.), the last great pagan philosopher of Antiquity and the most illustrious representative of Neo-Platonism (8). He is an unusually difficult writer, partly on account of his terse style, but chiefly because his system reaches the highest possible point of metaphysical abstraction. Moreover, his system is very remote from all present forms of Western theology. Nevertheless, its historical significance makes a brief discussion of it inevitable (9).

According to Plotinus the world is derived from a divine realm which consists in three 'hypostases': the One, Mind and Soul. Unlike the members of the Christian Trinity these are unequal. The One generates Mind, and Mind generates Soul; and just as Soul is inferior to Mind, so Mind is inferior to the One. In so far as the One is the ultimate reality and the source of everything else it is equivalent to the Christian God. Plotinus describes it in wholly negative terms. It entirely

59

transcends both being and thought. We cannot say that it 'is' or give any description of it. It is an absolutely simple, changeless self-identity to which no positive property can be ascribed. Even to call it 'one' is misleading, for the category of number (like all other categories) is inapplicable to it (10).

By an inner necessity the One expresses itself in lower forms of being, which, however, do not in any way diminish it (11). The first object of its self-expression is Thought or Mind, which contains in itself the ideal principles of all things and which contemplates both the One and itself. The second object is Soul, which relates the intelligible to the sensible worlds. Plotinus describes the derivation of Mind from the One through the metaphors of emanation and overflowing. 'The Intellectual-Principle stands as the image of the One, firstly because there is a certain necessity that the first should have its off-spring, carrying onward much of its quality, in other words that there be something in its likeness as the sun's rays tell of the sun' (12). Again, 'seeking nothing, possessing nothing, lacking nothing, the One is perfect and, in our metaphor, has overflowed, and its exuberance has produced the new: this product has turned again to its begetter and been filled and has become its contemplator' (13).

Plotinus thus envisaged the finite world as descending, in a series of decreasingly real emanations, from the One through Mind and Soul. The lowest stage is matter. Plotinus's teaching on matter is not entirely clear, but it seems to be this. On the one hand, since he regarded the physical world as emanating (however distantly) from the infinitely perfect One, he refused to follow Gnosticism in considering it to be evil (14). On the other hand he attributed evil to the formless potency of 'first' matter, which he thought of, Platonically, as underlying all material entities (15). This matter does not have independent existence; it exists only when combined with some positive power of being; but when so combined it has a destructive effect. Although it is in itself entirely negative, it has a positive capacity for limiting the good that flows from the divine realm.

No speculative and religious mind can fail to admire

Plotinus's system for its comprehensiveness, its subtlety, its originality and its spiritual power. Christian theists must be especially grateful for its emphasis on divine transcendence. Its lasting influence on St Augustine is fully comprehensible. Nevertheless it is exposed to the following metaphysical and religious criticisms.

1. Is Plotinus's view of the One meaningful? If we cannot make any positive statements about the One, how can we speak of it intelligibly? How can we distinguish between the One and sheer 'nothing'? This difficulty arises from any unqualified use of the 'negative way' (*via negativa*). Furthermore, Plotinus is bound to imply some knowledge of it in so far as he affirms that it *is* One (in contrast with the multiplicity of everything below it), and that all things flow from it as their undiminished Source.

Admittedly Plotinus sometimes appears to modify his negative approach, as in the following passage:

> Once more, we must be patient with language; we are forced for reasons of exposition to apply to the Supreme terms which strictly are ruled out; everywhere we must read 'So to speak' The Good, then, exists; it holds its existence through choice and will, conditions of its very being: yet it cannot be a manifold; therefore the will and the essential being must be taken as one identity; the act of the will must be self-determined and the being self-caused; thus reason shows the Supreme to be its own Author. For if the act of will springs from God Himself and is as it were his operation and the same will is identical with his essence, He must be self-established. He is not, therefore, 'what He has happened to be' but what He has willed to be (16).

In the conclusion of this passage Plotinus seems to be at one with Christian theists in affirming that mind and will actually inhere in God in a manner appropriate to his self-existence. But his initial *caveat* ('so to speak') must be taken, in the total context of the 'Enneads', to mean that any attribution of any positive term to God is no more than a concession to the weakness of our finite minds. Thus in a

61

slightly earlier passage, having stated that the One is completely undefinable, he is driven to the following paradox. The One 'is to be conceived as the total power towards things, supremely self-concentred, being what it wills to be or rather projecting into existence what it wills, itself higher than all will' (17).

2. The image of emanation is an untenable attempt to find a middle way between the theistic doctrine of creation and pantheism. Through the image Plotinus hoped to combine two incompatible beliefs — the belief that the One transcends the Many in its absolute simplicity and the belief that it is identical with the Many of which it is the source. Copleston states the matter thus:

> It is quite true that for Plotinus the world proceeds from God *secundum necessitatem naturae* and that he rejects free creation *ex nihilo*; but it should also be remembered that for him the prior Principle remains 'in its own place', undiminished and unimpaired, always transcending the subordinate being. The truth of the matter would seem to be that, while rejecting free creation out of nothing on the ground that this would involve change in God, Plotinus equally rejects a fully pantheistic self-canalisation of the Deity in individual creatures, a self-diremption of God. In other words he tries to steer a middle course between theistic creation on the one hand and a fully pantheistic or monistic theory on the other hand. We may well think that (since an ultimate dualism does not enter into the question) no such compromise is possible (18).

3. The role of 'matter' has always been regarded as a perplexing element in Plotinus's system. I cannot see how it is possible to avoid the following antinomy. If matter is entirely indeterminate, how does it differ from sheer non-being? The only answer to this question is to distinguish between a form of non-being ($\mu\grave{\eta}$ ὄν) which is a mere, formless potentiality, and sheer 'nothing' (οὐκ ὄν). I can only repeat that I find the first of these ideas quite unintelligible. To speak of a potentiality which is not the potentiality of *something* is surely meaningless (19). Yet if matter is a

determinate power, a characterisable activity, Plotinus is committed to the dualism that he rejects. Moreover if this power is evil he is committed to the Gnostic type of dualism that he found especially repulsive.

4. The Plotinian One cannot satisfy any of those religious needs that are satisfied by theism. Admittedly Plotinus wrote of, and apparently experienced, ecstatic union with the One; but this union is purely the result of intellectual contemplation. The One remains entirely impersonal, and so entirely indifferent to mankind. It cannot reveal itself; it cannot love; it cannot enter into any kind of personal relationship with anyone. Consequently it cannot become the object of worship. The difference between Plotinus and his Christian disciple St Augustine here has been aptly stated by Paul Henry thus:

> In the passage of Augustine's 'Confessions' which is most directly inspired by the 'Enneads', the words of Plotinus are: 'Now call up all your confidence; you need a guide no longer; strain and see.' And Augustine, quoting from the Psalm, writes: 'I entered even into my inward self, Thou being my Guide, and able I was, for Thou wert become my Helper.' In this inversion of a thought essential to Plotinus lies all the distance between Neo-Platonic and Christian mysticism (20).

In spite of his close intellectual and spiritual affinity with Plotinus, Augustine modifies the latter's concept of the Absolute at two crucial points in order to bring it into line with Christian theology. God, for Augustine, is the personal Creator of the world; and he is the Saviour by whose grace alone men can be freed from their sins and brought to the glory of his presence.

Admittedly, some Christian mystics who have been influenced directly or indirectly by Plotinus have spoken of God as if he were an impersonal, formless Monad. The most obvious example is the pseudo-Dionysius (the so-called 'Areopagite') (21). Yet in the main tradition of Christian mysticism there is no confusion between the nameless One of

63

Plotinus and the personal God of Christianity (22). When Christian mystics speak of God through the 'apophatic' way (the *via negativa*), their utterances are to be judged in the total context of their prior faith in the personal God of Christian revelation. The infinite One whom they experience as the utterly transcendent Light that darkens intellectual understanding is the One in whom they have already believed as the Father of Jesus Christ (23).

Of these criticisms the most important for our purpose are the first and second. Plotinus's chief contribution to metaphysical theology is his apprehension of God's transcendence. Here much that he says is magnificently compelling. Yet he confronts us with an inconsistency and a problem. He is inconsistent in so far as he affirms on the one hand that the One is characterless and on the other hand that it possesses mental properties to an eminent degree. The problem is posed by the first of these affirmations. If we cannot offer any description of 'God' can we attach any significance to the term? Is there any difference between complete silence and complete agnosticism? The latter question is relevant to all extreme forms of the negative way (for example, to some forms of Hinduism and Buddhism). At any rate it is important to distinguish between the characteristically Neo-Platonic assertion that we cannot attribute any properties to God and the theistic assertion that we can atrribute them by analogy. Both Plotinus and Aquinas would agree that God is incomprehensible; but Aquinas would add that he is so in virtue of his infinite possession of those spiritual qualities which, on grounds of both reason and revelation, we ascribe to him. Basically, whereas Plotinus was content to say, in words derived from Plato, that the One is 'beyond being', Aquinas said that God *is* being in a self-existent form and that his self-existence determines the form of all his properties.

Next there are the metaphors of 'emanation' and 'over-flowing' which Plotinus uses to describe the relation between the One and subordinate grades of being. It is hard to see how the following antinomy can be evaded. Either we take the metaphors to mean God's act in creating the world out of nothing; or we take them to mean that God actually imparts a share of his being to the world. The first meaning implies a personal view of God that is incompatible with Plotinus's contention that God is wholly indescribable. The second meaning is very hard to square with Plotinus's contention that the One is not modified by anything that proceeds from it.

Both these problems will recur with reference to other thinkers and schools of thought in subsequent sections. In the next two sections I shall discuss pantheism and panentheism, which (so I have suggested) are the only alternatives to theism.

(c) Pantheism

'Pantheism' (which is derived from the Greek words for 'all' and 'God') signifies the belief that every existing entity is, in some sense, divine. Pantheists are 'monists' (a term derived from the Greek word for 'single' or 'alone'); they believe that there is only one Being, and that all other forms of reality are either modes (or appearances) of it or identical with it. Therefore, although pantheists differ among themselves at many points, they all agree in denying the basic theistic claim that God and the world are ontologically distinct.

I shall briefly summarise four main philosophical forms of pantheism (24).

The most influential form of pantheism in the Graeco-Roman world was Stoicism. The Stoics held that there is one Being, the cosmic *Logos* ('Reason') or *anima mundi*, ('Soul of the world') which they identified with Nature's basic elements (air and fire). Each person, they held, participates in this Logos through his own powers of reason. Sometimes they personified this Logos in order to satisfy religious and moral needs. Thus they called it Zeus, addressed prayers to it, and regarded submission to its providence as the sign of true wisdom.

Within the Christian era the purest instance of pantheism is the wholly *a priori* system of Spinoza (1632-77). Hence I

65

shall take him as my chief example. The basis of his thought is that there is only one (an infinite) substance — God. 'God I understand to be a being absolutely infinite, that is, a substance consisting of infinite attributes, each of which expresses eternal and infinite essence' (25). God's substance has two infinite attributes (extension and thought), of which all finite beings are modes. 'Extension and thought are either attributes of God or modifications of attributes of God' (26). We can speak of either God or Nature. Looked at from one side the Universe is creative; looked at from the other it is created. Consequently everything is absolutely determined by God's nature. 'All things must have followed of necessity from a given nature of God, and they were determined for existence or action in a certain way by the necessity of the divine nature' (27). Consequently human thoughts are the thoughts of God (28).

Although Spinoza's system is so speculative he intended it to have a practical effect. He writes of it thus in the concluding paragraph of part 2:

> It teaches us to act solely according to the decree of God and to be partakers of the divine nature, the more according as our actions are more perfect and more and more understand God. This doctrine, therefore, besides bringing complete peace to the mind, has this advantage also, that it teaches us in what consists our greatest happiness or blessedness, namely, in the knowledge of God, by which we are induced to do those things which love and piety persuade us.

In particular Spinoza urges his readers to love God. This, however, is a purely intellectual love. It is neither more nor less than a finite reflection of the infinite love with which God loves himself:

> The mental intellectual love/ towards God is the very love of God with which God loves himself, not in so far as he is infinite, but in so far as he can be expressed through the essence of the human mind considered under the species of eternity, that is, mental intellectual love towards God is part of the infinite love with which God loves himself (29).

66

The next great pantheist was Hegel (1770-1831). He differs from Spinoza chiefly in the fact that he interpreted the relation of God, or the Absolute, to the world in dynamic terms. The absolute develops itself, and comes to full self-consciousness, through historical events. History, in its dialectical movement of thesis—antithesis—synthesis, is the self-manifestation of God's infinite life. Hegel particularised this divine evolution to the extent of holding that its supreme exemplification was the German state of his day. He also maintained that his philosophical system was compatible with Christianity in so far as the Christian doctrine of the Incarnation symbolises the ideal of divine—human unity to which all men (*qua* concrete expressions of the universal Spirit) approximate.

In the East the most sophisticated forms of pantheism are those constructed by Hindu thinkers. The basic theme (derived from the non-dualistic strain in the Upanishads) is that there is one Supreme Being (Brahman) which is entirely beyond human understanding, and which (like the Neo-Platonic One) can be spoken of only through the *via negativa*. The relation of the one Brahman to the world is variously expressed. Sometimes the relation is stated in terms similar to those used by the Western pantheists I have mentioned. Finite entities are not unreal; but they are real only as modes of the Absolute. However, according to Hindu monism in its most extreme form (as represented by Sankara), every human soul is identical with Brahman, and the sensible world of separate objects is an 'illusion' (*maya*) (30).

All these thinkers hold that there is only one Reality and, therefore, that finite things and persons exist only in so far as they express its nature. But the following points must be noted.

(a) The One is not always called God. The Hindus call it Brahman. F. H. Bradley called it the Absolute and opposed it to the personal God of Christianity. Hence 'monism' is more accurate than 'pantheism' as an all-inclusive description. The justification for 'pantheism' is that the One, by whatever name it is called, is the metaphysical equivalent to the God of theism.

67

(b) Monists differ in the status which they accord to finite entities. They are all bound to deny that these entities are substantially independent of God (or therefore of each other). But whereas Spinoza and Hegel held that the Infinite diversifies itself in finite objects (so that the latter are real aspects of its being or phases in its self-development), Bradley held that the world of 'the many' is merely an 'appearance' of an Absolute that is a pure, ineffable Unity. Sankara went even further in maintaining that the world of separate objects is unreal — a sheer illusion.

(c) Consequently, monists differ in the accounts they give concerning human knowledge of the One. According to Spinoza and Hegel this knowledge is a rational comprehension of the world as a divine unity-in-diversity. But according to Bradley it is a supra-rational recognition that all appearances are somehow transfigured in the Absolute. According to Sankara it is the realisation of one's spiritual identity with Brahman.

(d) Monists are bound to give, or imply, differing evaluations of the world. Spinoza and Hegel were obviously obliged to ascribe an infinite value to it. Nature for Spinoza, and History for Hegel, constitute the immediate content of God's being. But for Bradley neither nature nor history can have more than a limited reality.

All monists, then, can be called pantheists in so far as they hold that everything is either unreal or real to the extent that it is the self-expression of the Absolute. The differences between the various forms of monism are negligible when compared with the difference between all these forms and theism, which rests on the affirmation that all creatures are substantially distinct from the Creator.

The attractions of pantheism are many. First, it can offer both intellectual and spiritual satisfaction. Thus Spinoza's system has a beautiful coherence and clarity that is reflected in its deductive, quasi-mathematical mode of expression. Another kind of intellectual satisfaction can be derived from Bradley's postulation of a supra-rational Absolute in which all contradictions disappear. Similarly Sankara's doctrine of a qualityless Brahman with which each human soul is identical

68

furnishes a metaphysical basis for mystical experience of a monistic kind. In these and other ways the pantheistic belief in an ultimate Unity in which all separate and contrary elements are reconciled brings peace and assurance to the distracted and doubting mind.

Again, many forms of pantheism give a wholly new and immediately divine significance to Nature and History. For Spinoza Nature *is* God, and for Hegel History *is* the Absolute. Everything that occurs in Nature or History is an aspect of God or a phase of his self-development. Pantheism abolishes the theistic distinction between the Creator and the creature, the sacred and the secular, the finite and the infinite; and in so doing it abolishes the theistic concept of mediation. Whereas the theist claims that God providentially orders the world through his transcendent power, the pantheist affirms that the ordering of the world is one with the order of God's own nature. Consequently whereas the theist claims that we can see a divine significance in the world only in so far as we refer it indirectly to the transcendent mystery of a God whose mind no man can know, pantheists of a Spinozistic or Hegelian type affirm that this significance is directly revealed in the structure of the world itself.

In particular pantheism gives rational confirmation to the sense of unity with Nature which so many people of widely differing backgrounds have experienced. From the most primitive vegetation rites to the most sophisticated poetry there is a vast and varied testimony to the fact that the human mind has a spontaneous tendency to feel a oneness with natural phenomena, and to see in them a manifestation of the Spirit in which they too participate. This feeling and this vision constitute a perennial strand in 'natural piety'. At the same time pantheists can give a unique significance to man. They can assert that although the divine Spirit expresses itself to some degree in all finite entities it expresses itself supremely in man, in whom (to use Hegelian terms) it reaches the final point of its self-development.

However, pantheism is exposed to the following objections, which seem to me to be fatal.

1. If 'God' (*theos*) is identical with the Universe (*to pan*)

it is merely another name for the Universe. It is therefore bereft of any distinctive meaning; so that pantheism is equivalent to atheism. When finite things are added together they are merely a finite collection; and any unity they have is a finite unity. In any case there are no grounds for supposing that the universe constitutes (even finitely) a single 'super-thing' (analogous to a tree) or a single 'super-person' (analogous to a man).

Yet if God to any extent transcends the world — if there is any element in his being that is not contained in the world — pantheism, in the strict sense, is false. And that God to some extent transcends the world is implied by most pantheists. Merely to speak of the world as the self-expression of the One is to imply that the One has a separate nature to express. The same criticism applies to any other term of relationship — to (logical) 'explication' or (historical) 'self-development' (31).

2. The idea that the world is a self-expression of God is incompatible with his infinity or self-existence. If God shares his being with the world he must be limited by it. Alternatively, if the world is (as it manifestly is and must be) contingent, and if it is a part of God, he cannot be necessary. To say that the same being is both necessary and contingent is as self-contradictory as it is to say that the same figure is both a circle and a square.

This self-contradiction emerges clearly from the following summary of Spinoza's monism given by Stuart Hampshire:

God or Nature is a free and originating cause, and the only free, because the only self-creating, cause; in so far as we think, as we always can, of God or Nature as the free and self-creating cause, we think of Nature, in Spinoza's phrase, as *Natura Naturans*, Nature actively creating herself and deploying her essential powers in her infinite attributes and in the various modes of these attributes. But we can also think of Nature (and this is the more general connotation of the word outside Spinoza's philosophy) as the system of what is created. Nature is conceived in its passive capacity, as an established system, or as *Natura*

70

Naturata, in Spinoza's phrase. Throughout Spinoza's philosophy use is made of this difficult device of conceiving what is in essence or reality the same thing, as manifesting itself in two different ways, or as having two different aspects (a vague word which one is sometimes driven to use in this context). It is equally correct to think of God or Nature as the unique creator (*Natura Naturans*) and as the unique creation (*Natura Naturata*); it is not only correct, but necessary to attach both of these complementary meanings to the word, neither being complete, or even possible, as a conception of Nature without the other (32).

Hampshire underestimates the tension in Spinoza's thought when he refers to the identification of the two Natures as 'a difficult device' which can be overcome by a vague use of the word 'aspect' (which is one of these words that are fatally accessible in moments of metaphysical desperation). It is surely a blatant self-contradiction to affirm of the same X that it is both self-existent and contingent, both infinite and finite, both Creator and created. The use of 'aspects' is thoroughly misleading for two conclusive reasons. First, Nature does not 'look' necessary; it looks entirely contingent. Secondly, if the same thing 'looks' as if it has mutually exclusive properties (like the notorious straight stick which looks bent in water), we assume that it cannot 'really' (*per se*) possess both these properties. The only way out of this logical impasse is to affirm (as panentheists affirm) either that there is an element (or hidden 'core') in God's self-existent being that is untouched by the contingent world or (paradoxically) that his necessity *consists in* his responsiveness to the world; so that he is necessarily all that he will become. For the moment I am concerned only with the unqualified Spinozistic (and so classically monistic) claim that the same Being is, without any qualification, both the one, infinite, self-existent Creator and the multiple world of finite, dependent and created entities.

3. Pantheism fails to explain our awareness of distinctness

and autonomy in things and persons. Our total experience of both personal and sub-personal entities is pervaded by the conviction that each is an independent form of existence. This conviction is immediately and uniquely present in each person's self-consciousness, whereby each is aware of himself as distinct from (and *therefore* capable of relating himself to) other persons. Pantheists can give one of two accounts of selfhood and thinghood. Both accounts are wholly unconvincing. According to the first account (available to those who adopt a rational form of pantheism), although each person is a mode of God each possesses a form of selfhood appropriate to this modality; each is a *self-conscious* mode. But this is absurd for three reasons. First, to speak of a self-conscious mode, or aspect, is a self-contradiction; it is like saying that 'a side of a large house' is equivalent to 'a small house'. Secondly, if we are self-conscious modes, why are we not conscious of being so? How did this metaphysical amnesia arise and (yet more seriously) come to pervade and dominate our whole experience? Thirdly, it is inconceivable how the Universal Self could include finite selves. A's thought, simply because it is A's, *cannot* include, though it may coincide with, B's thought. Their mutual exclusion belongs (ontologically) to the nature, and so (logically) to the definition, of selfhood. Yet if we say (with Bradley) that finite selves are mere 'appearances', or *a fortiori* (with Sankara) that they are illusory, we must face two unanswerable objections. First, how could such an appearance or illusion of multiplicity be created by a unitary Absolute? Secondly, if our selfhood is illusory, or even if it is only semi-real, none of our individual statements can be true — least of all our statements concerning a supposed Absolute.

4. Pantheists are bound to find the fact of evil (and especially moral evil) an enormous embarrassment. It is difficult enough to square this fact with belief in an omnipotent and infinitely loving Creator. It is much more difficult to square it with the view that an evil world is an actual expression of God's perfect nature. There is in fact only one solution — to affirm that evil too is merely 'apparent'. What seems to us, from our partial standpoint,

72

evil is really (when viewed *sub specie aeternitatis*) a necessary element in the good of the Whole. But this view is contrary to our conviction that although good may be brought out of evil the latter (even if it can be defined as a 'privation of good') is fully, and often hideously, real.

5. The religious possibilities of pantheism are strictly limited. Although it can permit reverence for, and even a quasi-mystical union with, Nature *qua* divine, it has no place for salvation, prayer, or any personal relationship between God and man. Stoic 'Providence' is another word for 'Fate'. Spinoza's 'intellectual love of God' is far removed from Platonic *eros*, and even farther from Christian *agape*; it is simply the mind's desire for self-identification with the determined order of things.

In the preceding critique I have assumed that a theory (in this case Spinozistic pantheism) is refuted if it is shown to be self-contradictory. But W. T. Stace, is his 'Mysticism and Philosophy', maintains that pantheistic attributions of contrary attributes to God (or the Absolute) are valid. He claims that although the laws of logic are applicable to finite entities they are inapplicable to the infinite One. Of the One we can say, without qualification, that it is both personal and impersonal, both other than the world and identical with it, both characterised by evil and not characterised by it. I am totally unable to understand this view. If (as Stace — in my view rightly — holds) the laws of logic are also laws of reality I cannot see how we can make any exception. Stace's attempt to justify the exception is an evasion. On p. 267 he says that 'if 'A is B' is a meaningful statement, and if 'A is not B' is also meaningful, it is impossible that the connective 'and' placed between them should render the conjunction of the two meaningful statements meaningless'. However, as H. D. Lewis observes (33), the conjunction is crucial; it constitutes the core of the objection.

Admittedly the Christian theist makes statements (for example that God's almighty love is compatible with the fact of evil, or that Jesus was both God and Man) which are paradoxical in the sense that they *seem* to be contrary to reason. Admittedly too some theologians (notably

Kierkegaard) have held that they actually are so. But the main tradition of Christian theism has been devoted to showing that the apparent contradictions are not real. Thus Christian theodicy is aimed at showing that sin and suffering are compatible with belief in God's omnipotence and love. Again, Christian theologians have continually tried to show that the union of Godhood and manhood in Christ is, though a mystery, consonant with all that we know concerning the divine and human natures.

It is impossible to prove the universal validity of logical laws; for any proof of anything involves their application. In fact Stace himself presupposes their application to the very sphere (the Absolute) to which he says they are inapplicable. He presupposes the law of the excluded middle in so far as he assumes that the Absolute either does or does not possess contrary properties. He presupposes the law of contradiction in so far as he assumes that the Absolute cannot both be and not be self-contradictory. Without these assumptions he could not distinguish between pantheism and theism, or, therefore, argue for the former against the latter.

I therefore maintain that although pantheism has received so many impressive formulations, and although it is both intellectually and spiritually attractive on the grounds I stated, it is exposed to grave and (in my opinion) fatal objections. Taken strictly it is equivalent to atheism; it involves a self-contradiction in its claim that the same Being is both one and many, both infinite and finite; it violates our pervasive sense of individuality or personal distinctness; it denies the full reality of evil; and it excludes some of the most important elements in religious experience. I shall re-examine it in Chapter 3 (with reference to some of the thinkers I shall discuss).

Finally, it is necessary to distinguish between pantheism and panentheism. Pantheism (which is derived from the Greek words for 'all' and 'God') means, strictly, the view that God is everything and everything is God. Panentheism (which is derived from the Greek words for 'all', 'in' and 'God') is defined thus in the 'Oxford Dictionary of the Christian Church': 'the belief that the Being of God includes and

74

penetrates the whole universe, so that every part of it exists in him, but (against pantheism) that his being is more than, and is not exhausted by the universe'.

This definition applies to many of the statements made by so-called 'pantheists' or 'monists'. Almost all monists imply at some point that God possesses some degree of 'otherness'. Thus Spinoza, although he identifies God with Nature, implies an element of transcendence in God in so far as he affirms that all things are necessitated by God, and that God loves himself through finite selves. Similarly Hegel speaks in some places as if God transcended the world, although in other places he asserts that God and the world are identical.

However, panentheism is not necessarily monistic. One could hold that God 'includes' and 'penetrates' the world without also holding that the world is a self-expression of his nature, a part of his substance. It would be possible to maintain that God creates the world or that the world, in at least some of its aspects, exists independently of him. In fact the most influential contemporary form of panentheism (which I shall examine in the next section) is non-monistic.

(d) Process theology

The term 'process theology' is applied to the theological speculations produced by a group of twentieth-century thinkers of whom the most illustrious are A. N. Whitehead and Charles Hartshorne. They believe that the idea of 'process' or 'becoming' must be taken as the chief category for interpreting the nature of both the world and God. Whereas classical theists see in God a pure Actuality who stands in opposition to the world of change, these thinkers see in him (or at least an aspect of him) the supreme exemplification of the capacity for growth that characterises creatures. In their view, just as a human person develops through his response to his environment, so too does God.

Process theology has points of resemblance to three of the systems I have examined. It resembles theism in so far as these theologians speak of God in personal terms; it resembles Plato's doctrine of a finite God in so far as they regard God as imposing form on a matter that exists independently of him; it resembles Hegel's panentheism in so far as they hold that God, in the process of self-development, includes and permeates the universe. The two main distinctive elements in their thought are these. First, most panentheists are monists; they hold that God, though partly other than the world, communicates his substance to it. But Whitehead and Hartshorne are not monists. While maintaining that God includes and penetrates the world, they also maintain that he and the world are substantially distinct. Secondly, although Hegel (and other thinkers I shall examine) imply that an aspect of God's nature is separate from the world, they do not make a systematic attempt to specify this aspect or to relate it to the aspect that is immanent in the world. Whitehead and Hartshorne, however, distinguish sharply between these aspects. Their chief claim to theological originality consists in the rigour and subtlety with which they make this distinction. In this section I shall deal briefly with those elements in their thought which coincide with theories I have already discussed. I shall devote my attention chiefly to the original element I have just stated.

My discussion of Whitehead must be preceded by a *caveat*. Next to F. H. Bradley he is beyond doubt the greatest metaphysician who has written in the English language in this century. I shall be considering only a fraction of his writings. My aim is solely to determine the essence of his views on God. Readers who wish for a full exposition of his thought should consult the works mentioned in my Bibliography. I shall discuss two of his works — 'Religion in the Making' (34) and 'Process and Reality' (35).

In 'Religion in the Making' Whitehead objects to classical theism on five grounds. First, if God is infinite he is unknowable (36). Secondly, his existence cannot be proved (37). Thirdly, if we say that God is omnipotent we inevitably view him in terms of power rather than of goodness, and regard fear rather than love as the appropriate response to him (38). Fourthly, 'to be an actual thing is to be limited' (p.

76

150). Fifthly, if God were infinite he would be evil as well as good (39).

Hence Whitehead advocates belief in a God who is finite and who, like Plato's Demiurge, imparts form to independently existing flux. God is an actual, non-temporal entity who 'imposes ordered balance on the world' (p. 94). Equally he gives to the world such value as it possesses. God 'is complete in the sense that his vision determines every possibility of value. Such a complete vision co-ordinates and adjusts every detail' (pp. 53-4). God does not make the world 'out of nothing'; he confers harmony and worth on a world of self-creating creatures (40). He is the formal but not the efficient cause of everything (41).

Moreover, Whitehead's theology is panentheistic; for he affirms that God both includes and permeates the world. Thus on p. 98 he writes: 'Since God is actual he must include in himself a synthesis of the total universe.' Correspondingly on p.156 he states that 'the world lives by the incarnation of God in itself'. But we must always remember that Whitehead (who is here followed by the other writers I shall discuss in this chapter) is not a monist. He and they constantly affirm that God's being is distinct from the being of the world.

In this book Whitehead expresses many truths that belong to the essence of personal theism. He asserts that God is to be understood primarily in terms of love; that he is the cause of Nature's order; and that his ultimate aim is to create elements of eternal value out of the fleeting occasions of this perishable world. But his concept of a finite God is exposed to the criticisms that I have already stated. Furthermore he does not consider the answers that can be given to the objections he brings against classical theism (42).

I turn now to 'Process and Reality', which is the most impressive of Whitehead's metaphysical writings and the one in which his concept of God is most fully expressed. Here too he states the most original element in his theology. This is his view that God's being has two poles or aspects — a 'primordial' nature (which is his nature in himself) and a 'consequent' nature (which is constituted by his response to and inclusion of the world). In place of classical theists' belief in one divine nature that is identical with existence Whitehead postulates two natures, of which one is created by finite occurences and which is therefore characterised by process or becoming.

In his primordial aspect God 'is the unlimited conceptual realisation of the absolute wealth of potentiality' (p. 486). As such he is 'deficiently actual' in two ways: his feelings are merely conceptual and he lacks consciousness (ibid.). As such too he is both the world's formal cause (for he ensures 'the relevance of eternal objects to the process of creation') (pp. 486-7), and the world's final cause (for he is related to the world as 'the lure for feeling' and the 'object of desire') (p. 487) (43). Whitehead sums up his views on God's primordial nature by saying that it is 'free, complete, eternal, actually deficient and unconscious' (p. 489).

God's consequent nature, by contrast, 'originates with physical experience derived from the temporal world, and then acquires integration with the primordial side. It is determined, incomplete, everlasting, fully actual, and conscious. His necessary goodness expresses the determination of his consequent nature' (p. 489). Through this nature God 'saves the world as it passes into the immediacy of his own life' (p. 490). By being part of this nature the world achieves 'objective immortality' (p. 491). 'The theme of Cosmology, which is the basis of all religions, is the story of the dynamic effort of the World passing into everlasting unity, and of the static majesty of God's vision, accomplishing its purpose of completion by absortion of the World's multiplicity of effort' (p. 494).

Whitehead then expresses this 'dipolar' (44) concept of God by means of the following 'group of antitheses whose apparent self-contradiction depends on neglect of the diverse categories of existence' (p. 492):

It is as true to say that God is permanent and the World is fluent, as that the World is permanent and God is fluent.

It is as true to say that God is one and the World many, as that the World is one and God many.

It is as true to say that, in comparison with the World, God is actual eminently, as that, in comparison with God, the World is actual eminently.

It is as true to say that the World is immanent in God, as that God is immanent in the World.

It is as true to say that God transcends the World, as that the World transcends God.

It is as true to say that God creates the World, as that the World creates God.

Whitehead's dipolarism invites the following queries.

1. According to Whitehead God's primordial nature is deficiently actual in so far as its feelings are merely conceptual and it is unconscious. But what is a 'conceptual' feeling? Also if God *qua* primordial is unconscious, how can he impose pattern on the world of flux? How too can he be 'complete' if he is 'deficient'? Does his 'completeness' consist in sheer potentiality?

2. In what mode or modes does God include the world within his 'consequent' nature? Whitehead suggests that God abstracts everything that is of value in the world and absorbs it into his own life. But 'inclusion' and 'absorption' are two different ideas. Moreover how is God's consequent nature related to his primordial nature? Whitehead says that the former is 'integrated' into the latter; but he does not explain the mode of integration.

3. Is the self-contradiction contained in Whitehead's antitheses merely apparent (as he claims) or is it real? It seems to me that if God is conceived as a Demiurge and if he is regarded as one who, in his consequent nature, develops in response to the world that he includes, these antitheses are, though paradoxical, not self-contradictory. The only possible exception is the third antithesis, where everything depends on the meaning of 'eminently'. If it means (as its scholastic usage suggests) 'perfectly' or 'necessarily' it is obviously inapplicable to the world. But what else can it mean? In any case the real difficulty is constituted by the properties of God's primordial nature. Primordially God, according to Whitehead, is non-temporal and complete. Yet these properties cannot be ascribed to the world. Moreover Whitehead does not explain how we can consistently affirm that they

coexist with those mutually limiting properties that God's consequent nature and the world have in common.

I shall pursue these queries (and especially the third) with reference to the writings of Charles Hartshorne and Schubert Ogden. Hartshorne has developed Whitehead's dipolarism from a purely philosophical standpoint. He has also attempted to defend it against the charge of self-contradiction. Ogden has stated it more briefly from a theological point of view. Hartshorne, after an ecstatic tribute to Whitehead, endorses the latter's view of God in these words:

> The foregoing passages seem to make it very clear that Whitehead fully accepts the five factors which we have specified as essential to the divine nature: eternity, temporality, consciousness, world knowledge, and world inclusion. God as primordial is strictly eternal in the sense of being immutable and ungenerated. God as consequent is 'fluent', reaches no final completion, contains succession, and is ever in 'process' of further creation (45).

Since Hartshorne's panentheism is so subtle, intricate and (I may assume) strange to many of my readers, I shall begin by quoting two passages from his writings, and a third passage from a book by Ogden. Both the first and second passages are taken from Hartshorne's 'Reality as Social Process' (46). On p. 23 he writes:

> The common saying, 'the God of philosophy is a quite different thing from the God of religion', is now antiquated, or at least, must be given a partly new meaning; since philosophy, in a long list of its modern and especially recent representatives, has for reasons of its own criteria of intelligibility made the great transition from a conception of God as devoid of relativity and *becoming* to the conception of him as in his full actuality the supreme relativity and *becoming*, the supreme subject of social relationships and interactions — though not, for all that, without an aspect of eternity, necessity, absoluteness, and independence (47).

80

Later in 'Reality as Social Process' (p. 116) Hartshorne gives an analysis of the grades of being. This is how he describes the highest Grade — God:

Highest Grade: Superiority to *All* Others, Transcendent or *Perfect* Being.
R. *Relative* (in eminent sense; super-relative): the *reflexive form*.
The concrete maximum; the self-surpassing surpasser of all. (God as self-contrasting life, process, or personality).
A. *Absolute* (in eminent sense): the *non-reflexive* form.
The abstract maximum; the self-unsurpassing surpasser of all others. (God as mere self-identical essence abstracted from the fullness of his accidents, the contingent contents of his awareness.)

Ogden, having stated the difficulty that philosophers have found in relating the finite to the infinite, writes:

But, on the dipolar view of God outlined here, this 'problem of synthesis' seems at last to have found a solution — and that in a way which is as far removed from classical pantheism as from its traditional theistic alternative. By conceiving God as infinite personal existence or creative becoming, one can assert God's independence of the actual world (in his abstract identity) without saying he is wholly external to it, and one can affirm his inclusion of the actual world (in his concrete existence) without denying that the world as actual is completely contingent and radically dependent on him as its sole necessary ground (48).

The grounds on which Hartshorne and Ogden posit dipolarity in God are mainly three.
(a) Dipolarity (as the preceding quotation from Ogden shows) is held to solve the perennial problem of the relation between the One and the Many, the infinite and the finite. Panentheism can be represented as a *via media* between an untenable monopolar theism on the one hand and an equally

81

untenable pantheism on the other. Theism posits a paradoxical relation between an infinite Creator and his finite creatures; pantheism solves the paradox by attenuating or abolishing the reality of finite beings; panentheism gives the only adequate answer by affirming the coexistence in God of the One and the Many, the infinite and the finite, being and becoming, necessity and dependence, eternity and temporality.

(b) Hartshorne insists that God cannot be personal if he is regarded as being incapable of passivity (that is, change in response to his environment), and plurality (that is, internal differentiation). We consider a right balance between activity and passivity, unity and plurality to be a sign of human excellence; therefore, if God is personal, we must consider it to be a sign of divine excellence also. We admire human persons to the extent that they combine force of character with adaptability, and self-consistency with a variety of functions. So too these must constitute our ground for worshipping God — provided that, while he surpasses himself through his responsiveness to the world, he is not surpassed by anything in the world (49).

(c) In particular, Hartshorne maintains that the self-sufficient, changeless God of classical theism cannot possess the property of love that Christian theists attribute to him. If God is love he must be a 'social' being. He (like any member of human society) must be affected by the objects of his love; he must grow in personality through his response to them; he must be pained by their sufferings and enriched by their achievements. If he did not need his human creatures for the completion of his being he would not have any reason for creating them. 'A being which contains, in sheer independence of others, all possible perfection and value must surely know better than to clutter up existence with beings which can add nothing to the value that would exist without them' (50).

In spite of the ingenuity of Hartshorne's arguments, panentheism cannot, in my opinion, survive the following objections.

First, and basically, dipolarism is self-contradictory. The
82

idea of the infinite by definition excludes the idea of the finite; the idea of the eternal by nature excludes the idea of the temporal; the idea of absolute necessity by nature excludes the idea of dependence. Panentheists are aware of this objection, but their attempts to answer it are, I think, inadequate.

The first answer consists in distinguishing between an aspect of God's being (corresponding to Whitehead's 'primordial nature') that is necessary, and an aspect (corresponding to Whitehead's 'consequent nature') that is dependent. Thus Ogden, following Hartshorne, distinguishes between God's 'abstract identity' (in which he is necessary) and his 'concrete existence' (in which he is dependent). I find this terminology unintelligible. What can 'abstract identity' mean? 'Abstract' has a logical, not an ontological, reference; it designates concepts, not entities. To speak of an abstract entity is nonsense (unless one means an *ens rationis* − an abstract idea considered merely as an object of the intellect). It may be said that 'abstract identity' here means God's necessity considered in isolation from all else in his being or reality. But this is an untenable notion for at least three reasons. First, the idea of necessity as a 'core' in God's being that is untouched by his other properties is meaningless. Secondly, the idea of God's 'necessity' entails the identity of his essence with his existence. God can be necessary if, and only if, he is all that he is (or could be) simultaneously. Thirdly, what is the relation between God's non-dependent 'abstract identity' and his dependent 'concrete existence'? Does the identity not 'exist'? And is not the concrete existence self-identical? It is very hard to resist the conclusion that all this is sheer word-spinning.

This conclusion is reinforced by Hartshorne's attempt to reconcile the idea of God's 'absolute' transcendence as the self-unsurpassing maximum, with the idea of his 'relative' transcendence as the self-surpassing surpasser of all. 'Through such self-excelling', Hartshorne writes, 'the most excellent being changes, not into a more excellent being, but into a more excellent state of the *same* being' (51). I find it impossible to conceive how any entity could achieve a better state

83

without becoming a better being. What is a 'state' except a state *of* being? And what is any being apart from its states? Even according to strict Thomism essence and existence are, though notionally separable, ontologically united even in creatures in whom essence is a mode of existing. And this is only commonsense. To say that a person's being is ontologically separate from his form of being is nonsense. It is doubly nonsense if the being is defined as an *ens perfectissimum*.

In attempting to rebut the charge that dipolarity involves self-contradiction Hartshorne writes as follows:

> But is not such double predication contradictory? The answer is that there is no law of logic against attributing contrasting predicates to the same individual, provided they apply to diverse aspects of this individual. Thus a man may be 'simple' in his fundamental intention but 'complex' in the details of his actions and perceptions. Of course, if there be no diversity of aspects in deity — because of his oft-vaunted 'simplicity' — then indeed he cannot be both absolute and relative. But the assumption of sheer simplicity is itself a monopolar one, and so it would beg the question to object to the dipolar view on this ground. In that aspect of deity to which 'One' exclusively applies, of course, there is not a diversity of factors; but in the aspect to which 'Many' applies, there is (52).

This answer is inadequate on two grounds. First, a human being's intention is finite; it shares the finitude of the person himself. But God's intention, in its primordial side, is infinite; it is absolute, uncreated and eternal. Secondly, a person's intention does not constitute a 'nature' that is separate from the 'nature' of the acts through which it is embodied. Both the intention and the acts constitute a single nature that is limited by, and relative to, its spatio-temporal environment.

Hartshorne's concluding sentence brings us back to objections I have already stated. It is appropriate to note again how easily the word 'aspect' can be used as a means of evading a metaphysical dilemma.

A yet more radical way out of the difficulty is taken by Hartshorne when he *identifies* God's 'absolute' with his 'relative' nature. Thus in 'The Logic of Perfection' (53) he identifies God's necessity with his 'infallible power to harmonize relativities in himself, to respond coherently to diverse stimuli' (pp. 136-7). Later he affirms that 'God is individuated by containing the world in himself' (p. 262). But how does God possess this necessity? Why *must* God adapt himself to the world? Again, why must he adapt himself to good, not to evil? Why must he become steadily better, not steadily worse? These questions cannot be answered unless God is self-existent goodness; and he cannot be this unless he actualises all his capacities simultaneously. Hartshorne, no less than Whitehead, makes God's existence irrational; for we can always ask what causes God to pass from phase 1 to phase 2. And this question has no answer if God's necessity is identified with his adaptability. Moreover, if God's individuality is constituted by his inclusion of the world, how does panentheism differ from pantheism? Finally, this identification of God's necessity and individuality with his responsiveness to the world is contrary to the clear-cut distinction that Hartshorne elsewhere posits between the absolute and relative 'aspects' of God's being.

Furthermore, the grounds on which panentheists posit dipolarity in God are, so I believe, invalid. The first and main ground — the claim that panentheism is more successful that theism or monism in relating the finite and the infinite — is obviously untenable if my preceding criticisms are correct. The second ground is surely a piece of gratuitous anthropomorphism. Because change and growth, in response to environment, characterise human personality, it does not follow that they also characterise the personality of God. On the contrary, their presence in our form of personality is an obvious sign of our finiteness. They are not essential to the spiritual qualities of which they are (in the finite case) conditions. The most perfect form of spiritual being would be one from which these conditions are absent. In any case Hartshorne's attempt to model the concept of divine personality univocally on the concept of its human counterpart founders on his view that God includes the world in his 'concrete reality'; for (as I observed in criticising pantheism) the idea of one self including another self is nonsensical (54).

The third ground for affirming dipolarity in God has considerable *prima facie* strength, and constitutes the most attractive aspect of panentheism. This is the claim that if God loves the world he must (a) need it, (b) grow in response to it, and (c) suffer with it. Yet I do not think that the first and second elements in this claim can be substantiated. In answer to (a) the Christian affirms the doctrine of the Trinity (according to which God's inner, self-sufficient life is itself a life of mutual self-giving that utterly excels all its finite copies) (55). Also the theist can reply that even on the human plane we admire acts of love to the extent that they exhibit altruism, that God's act in creating the world is the only act which can be *wholly* altruistic, and that though we cannot have a positive notion of his altruism, we can understand that it constitutes the perfect form of charity. In answer to (b) it is sufficient to repeat that if the world is created totally by God he *cannot* grow in response to it; for there is nothing in the world that does not already exist ideally in his mind.

On (c) I partly agree and partly disagree with Hartshorne. I agree that if God is love he must be affected by the evils that afflect mankind. The loving Creator shares the pains, as well as the joys, of his creatures. But I disagree that God, in thus sharing our experiences, grows in personal stature (as we thus grow through our sympathetic response to our fellow-men); for God is pure act, and he cannot be enriched by any creature.

In any case, Hartshorne's account of divine suffering is most unsatisfactory. According to him, although God suffers in his consequent nature he is untouched by suffering in his primordial nature, in which he 'forever enjoys the vision of his own necessary essence' and possesses 'a satisfaction that is untarnished' (56). Thus Hartshorne avails himself of an inherently unintelligible dichotomy in order to secure a core (or, to use his own word, 'aspect') of absolute impassibility in God. Yet he holds that not merely sympathy, but growth through sympathy, belongs to the essence of personality. Is, then, God's primordial nature non-personal?

Admittedly the idea of a suffering God is also hard to square with classical, so-called 'monopolar', theism. But classical theists who believe that God is capable of suffering do not divide the Godhead in a manner that is as unsatisfactory metaphysically as it is religiously. According to them it is the *whole* God who suffers. Moreover, although we cannot form an adequate idea of the manner in which God's sufferings are transfigured in his joy, we have pointers to this transfiguration in both human experience and the Johannine view of Christ's Passion as the supreme manifestation of God's 'glory'.

This critique of Hartshorne shows the importance of distinguishing between different senses of 'response', 'passivity' and 'passibility'. That God responds to men must be admitted by all Christian theists; for the admission is required by belief in petitionary prayer. But 'response' does not imply 'change'. On the contrary, Christians are committed to the belief that God's response to their prayers is determined by his changeless desire for, and knowledge of, their good. Nothing that creatures do, and nothing that happens to them, can cause any increase (or decrease) in this desire and knowledge. Christian prayer presupposes that God's mind and will are immutable. Even if we say (according to the interpretation of omniscience I offered) that God does not know future free choices in their concrete actuality, he knows them perfectly as possibilities; he is (as the Creator) wholly sovereign over them; so that he is necessarily and timelessly adapted to them and to all their consequences.

It is equally important to distinguish between different senses of 'passivity' and 'passibility'. According to all interpretations of Christian theism God is passive in three ways necessitated by his creation of spiritual beings: he receives their worship, he responds to their requests, and he co-operates with their free decisions. He is also passible in the sense that he experiences the love and joy that he is within his essence. I have also claimed that he is passible in the sense that he experiences pain and sorrow on account of evil.

87

However God is not passive in the distinctive sense affirm-ed by panentheists. He cannot change for better (or for worse) in response to creaturely activities. Thus even if (as I have maintained) he suffers on account of finite evil, his sufferings do not modify his perfection. They cannot make him more loving (for he is self-existent love); they cannot make him more submissive (for there is no one to whom he must submit); they cannot enlarge his perspective (for he already sees everything *sub specie aeternitatis*). And if suffering cannot ennoble him it cannot degrade him. He remains ever the same — absolutely perfect in wisdom, goodness and power.

I therefore conclude that dipolarism is logically untenable. In all its forms it involves self-contradiction. The same being cannot be both absolute and relative, both changeless and changing, both eternal and temporal. Admittedly, panen-theists like Whitehead and Hartshorne are not *immediately* involved in self-contradiction, as are straightforward pan-theists like Spinoza; for they posit a substantial distinctness between God and the world by which he is affected. Admit-tedly too they concede a paradox (an *apparent* contradic-tion). But ultimately they are caught in the self-contradictuon that afflicts pantheists. The finite and the infinite can be rationally combined only in the theistic re-lation of created to Creator.

Finally, dipolarism cannot satisfy distinctively religious needs. I can best indicate its religious deficiency by two refer-ences to a paper by Hartshorne entitled 'Whitehead, the Anglo-American Philosopher-Scientist' (57). On p. 167 he affirms that by contributing to God's consequent nature we 'enrich the divine life itself'. He then quotes the Johannine statement that 'we love him because he first loved us'. On p. 170 he writes as follows of Whitehead's view that the world is immortalised in God's memory. 'The simplicity and clarity of this view seem to me sublime. It gives reality a means whereby it perpetually sums itself up, and preserves its achievements. 'O death, where is thy sting, O grave, where is thy victory?' '

Hartshorne's attempt to support Whitehead's doctrine by
88

an appeal to the New Testament is thoroughly misleading. The idea that we can enrich God's being is incompatible with the absolute adoration of God and the sense of absolute dependence on him that pervade the religion of the Bible. Also Whitehead's denial of personal immortality and his claim that finite experiences survive as elements in God's memory are incompatible with the Pauline passage that Hartshorne quotes. Religiously dipolarism is beyond doubt non-Christian.

Whether dipolarism is religiously appealing from a non-Christian standpoint I must leave others to decide. One thing at any rate is objectively clear. Dipolarism (like all concepts of a finite God) omits those elements which distinguish religious experience from all other experiences. Unless God is, without qualification, infinite there is no scope for the feeling of absolute dependence and the sense of the holy which Schleiermacher and Otto rightly took to be differentiating marks of the religious consciousness.

I shall now examine the thinkers whom I mentioned in my introduction. By means of this examination I hope to elucidate, interrelate, and assess more thoroughly the various forms of theology I have discussed.

Chapter 3

(a) Pringle-Pattison

I have chosen Pringle-Pattison's Gifford Lectures (1). as the first text to examine because it excellently illustrates the state of much philosophical theology in the first two decades of this century — just before the impact of Kierkegaard, Barth and neo-positivism. The two philosophers with whom Pringle-Pattison is chiefly concerned are Hegel and F. H. Bradley. His aim is to present a modified form of Hegelianism which will do justice to all aspects of both religious and non-religious experience. Whether he fulfils this aim is, as we shall see, doubtful.

Pringle-Pattison begins by expressing dissatisfaction with the theological conclusions of Hume and Kant. Hume's view that there *may* be a cosmic Designer is very far removed from the religious man's belief in God — a belief 'which, if true, must profoundly affect our whole view of the universe and our conduct in it' (p. 23). Kant, in his 'Critique of Practical Reason', related God to morality in a purely extrinsic manner which is equally inadequate. 'God seems to be introduced in Kant's moral theory almost as an after-thought, and he is connected with the [moral] law, not as its inspirer or author, but in the merely administrative capacity of Paymaster' (p. 35). Instead we should see our moral ideals as 'the immediate presence within us of a Spirit leading us into all truth and goodness' (p. 37).

Pringle-Pattison then criticises Kant, more generally, for driving a wedge between 'the objective certitude, *or knowledge*, attainable in the scientific sphere and the subjective certitude, or *faith*, on which our ethical postulates rest' (p. 47). This dichotomy is not confined to the 'Critique of Practical Reason'. 'A similar impression is produced by Kant's halting treatment of aesthetic experience and of the

90

organism in the 'Critique of Judgement'. While recognising in both cases a range of experience which his categories fail to express, he refuses to treat the aesthetic and the biological account of the phenomena as more than a subjective way of looking at facts which, were our analysis keen enough, might yet be reduced to instances of mechanical determination' (p. 50). But Nature cannot be exhaustively described in mechanistic terms; it demands an explanation in terms of a spiritual principle.

Pringle-Pattison's next chapter (4) is entitled 'The liberating influence of biology', in which his thesis is that 'the concentrated biological research of the last fifty years, while it has immensely extended our knowledge of the mechanics and the chemistry of organic processes, has strikingly failed to substantiate the mechanistic hypothesis from which most of the researchers started' (p. 71). In the course of evolution real differences emerge which cannot be fully explained in terms of their antecedent conditions. We cannot explain conscious organisms in terms of non-conscious ones; and we cannot explain any organism in terms of the inorganic state from which it arose. Moreover, it is illegitimate to appeal to a 'vital principle' conceived as somehow supplementing the material forces dealt with in physics and chemistry (2). Hence we must interpret the earlier through the later, the lower through the higher, and each separate element through the Whole of which it is a part and outside which it lacks a final significance. 'In the interpretation of any process, it is *the process as a whole* that has to be considered, if we wish to know the nature of the reality revealed in it. In other words, every evolutionary process must be read in the light of its last term. This is the true meaning of the profound Aristotelian doctrine of the Telos or End as the ultimate principle of explanation' (p. 106).

Pringle-Pattison then proceeds to claim (in chapter 6) that if we regard the world as a single, purposeful Whole we can adopt a 'realist' interpretation of knowledge; for man, being 'organic to the world', is capable of cognising its true nature. 'Each creature has its own world, in the sense that it sees only what it has the power of seeing; but what it apprehends, up to the limit of its capacity, is a true account of its environment' (p. 127). This thesis is affirmed even more explicitly on p. 129 thus: 'All idealism teaches the correlativity of subject and object; they develop *pari passu* keeping step together in as much as the objective world seems to grow in richness as we develop faculties to apprehend it. But all sane idealism teaches that, in such advance, the subject is not creating new worlds of knowledge and appreciation for himself, but learning to see more of the one world, 'which is the world of all of us.''

Pringle-Pattison further affirms that this unified, developing world-process is itself divine. Early in the book he says that the ultimate question facing philosophers is that 'of the divineness or the undivineness of the universe' (p. 40). He therefore feels free to speak of the Universe as a spiritual, conscious entity. Thus he describes man as 'the organ through which the universe beholds and enjoys itself' (p. 111). On p. 211 he expands this language: 'The rational being appears as the goal towards which Nature is working, namely, the development of an organ by which she may become conscious of herself and enter into the joy of her own being.' Consequently he sees an aspect of truth in Compte's religion of Humanity (p. 144).

The world is divine because it is the self-expression of God (or the Absolute) (3). Thus on p. 259 we read:

No act of creation is conceivable or possible which should extrude us from the life of God and place us, as solitary units, outside the courses of his being. The individual self, in other words, does not exist 'strong in solid singleness', like a Lucretian atom. The currents of the divine life course through it; it is open to all the influences of the universe. As we have already seen, how should we explain the fact of progress, if not by this indwelling in a larger life – this continuity with what is more and greater than ourselves? And it is from the fact that the finite individual is thus rooted in a wider life, to whose influences it remains throughout accessible, that those visitings of grace, of which the religious consciousness testifies, become most

92

easily intelligible — as well as those more violent upheavals of the personality as we have known it, in which, as religion says, the man is born again and becomes a new creature.

On this view God and man are necessarily correlative. Just as man exists through expressing the being of God, so God exists through this act of self-expression. 'As soon as we begin to treat God and man as two independent facts, we lose our hold upon the experienced fact, which is *the existence of the one in the other and through the other*' (p. 254). Pringle-Pattison states the same thesis on p. 315, where he writes that 'the infinite in and through the finite, the finite in and through the infinite — this mutual implication is the ultimate fact of the universe as we know it'.

The point that particularly needs to be stressed is that, according to Pringle-Pattison, God has no existence apart from his self-manifestation in the world. God and the world are coeternal. God is essentially Creator (4); and creation is an act whereby he imparts a share in his very substance to the creature. To suppose (according to classical theism) that God possesses a totally self-sufficient existence is to interpret him in terms of less than the highest that we know; for self-giving and finding oneself in others is the perfection of human life (5).

However, Pringle-Pattison rejects what he calls the 'lower Pantheism' which regards God as being completely and equally revealed in everything. His grounds for rejection are two. First, pure pantheism (according to which God and the world are identical) reduces 'God' to a mere class-name and so is equivalent to atheism. 'The doctrine of immanence becomes on these terms a perfectly empty affirmation; for the operative principle supposed to be revealed is simply the characterless unity of 'Being' in which the sum-total of phenomena is indiscriminately housed. The unity reached is the unity of a mere collection, and everything remains just as it was before. Such a pantheism is indistinquishable from the barest Naturalism' (p. 219). Secondly, pure pantheism obliterates distinctions of value. Pringle-Pattison writes thus of Spinoza on p. 221: 'His insistence on the universal and

93

thorough-going immanence of the divine causation exposed him to the accusation of abolishing the distinction between good and evil, and, indeed, of reducing all distinctions to one dead level of indifference.'

Pringle-Pattison is therefore better described as a panentheist than as a pantheist. Although he consistently maintains that the world is the self-expression of God, he also holds that there is an aspect of God's life which is entirely separate from and independent of the world. He affirms this explicitly in note E, where he answers some of his critics. 'My argument presupposes at every turn a comprehensive divine experience which is other than, and infinitely more than, that of any finite self or of all finite selves collectively, if their several contributions could be somehow pieced together' (p. 433).

As one would expect, Pringle-Pattison devotes several pages to a critique of Bradley's monism, which he finds unsatisfactory in two main respects. First, Bradley fails to explain 'how the bewildering mass of phenomenal diversity is harmonised, and its contradictions reconciled, in the Absolute' (p. 229). Secondly, Bradley, on the grounds of *a priori* speculation, reduces to the status of 'appearance' those elements in our experience which carry with them an immediate, self-authenticating guarantee of reality: 'It is an inversion of the true philosophic method to try to define the Absolute on the basis of the empty principle (6), and from the definition to reason *down* to the various phases of our actual experience, and to condemn its most characteristic features as 'irrational appearance' and 'illusion' ' (p. 230).

In particular Pringle-Pattison claims (with reference to Bosanquet as well as Bradley) that unqualified monism violates our persistent experience of ourselves and others as distinct persons. 'Finite centres', he writes, 'may 'overlap' indefinitely in content, but they cannot overlap at all in existence; their very *raison d'être* is to be distinct and, in that sense, separate and exclusive focalizations of a common universe' (p. 264). Individuals possess a substantival, not adjectival, form of being; each is a πρώτη οὐσία in Aristotle's sense (7). Consequently, the individuality of selves must be

94

preserved within the Absolute. Although God includes all persons he does not obliterate their distinctness, which is, not only an all-pervasive datum of ordinary experience, but also a requirement of the religious consciouness. 'The religious attitude — all that we mean by worship, adoration, self-surrender — is wholly impossible, if the selves are conceived as telephone wires along which the Absolute acts or thinks. As it has often been remarked, the system of Spinoza has no room in it for Spinoza himself and 'the intellectual love of God' with which he closes his 'Ethics' ' (p. 291).

Finally Pringle-Pattison claims that his panentheism is capable of including all the main Christian doctrines once they have been suitably reinterpreted. The spirit of Christianity requires, not the Jewish 'monarchical' view of a transcendent deity, but the Hegelian idea of a God who shares his nature with the world (8). Orthodox theologians have erred in limiting the Incarnation to one individual; for God is incarnate in the whole human race (9). The doctrines of the Atonement and the Trinity must be similarly re-expressed. 'Christ must die daily; the world is redeemed as well as created continually, and the whole life of God is poured into what we call our human 'Now' ' (p. 370). The doctrine of the Trinity is not 'a supra-rational mystery concerning the inner constitution of a transcendent Godhead', but 'the profoundest attempt to express the indwelling of God in man' (p. 410).

Pringle-Pattison thus hopes to retain all that is best in Hegelianism while conserving all that is true in theism (10). Unquestionably he has made many points of value. He has, in my opinion, shown that a purely mechanistic interpretation of evolution is inadequate; but this is a complicated subject which I cannot discuss here (11). His criticisms of Kant are acute, and his objections to pure monism (especially on the ground that it violates the distinctness of selves) are un-answerable. Moreover, his lectures contain many subsidiary insights of both a metaphysical and a religious nature. Thus I think he has provided valuable analogies to the manner in which the world's temporal processes are both retained and intuitively transcended in the divine consciousness (12).

95

Lastly, his philosophical learning is massive and (so far as I can discover) impeccable.

Nevertheless, deeply indebted though I am both to the book's matter and to its tone I think that it is exposed to the following queries and criticisms.

1. What is the content of God's independent nature? We are told that God possesses his own experiences which he does not share with the world; but what they are remains unclear. Consequently there is also a lack of clarity concerning the relation between God's transcendent being and his immanent self-expression. Since Pringle-Pattison both rejects the idea of a finite or evolving God (13) and affirms God's self-expression in the evolution of finite beings, he leaves us with only two possibilities. Either God is infinite and changeless in his transcendent aspect only, or he possesses these properties in his transcendent and immanent aspects equally. The first possibility, though less obviously objectionable than the second, is exposed to the difficulties I stated with reference to Hartshorne's form of panentheism. The second possibility constitutes, not a paradox, but a self-contradiction if (as Pringle-Pattison holds) the finite centres through which God expresses himself are fully real (14).

2. In particular, Pringle-Pattison's remarks on divine personality are ambiguous. On the one hand he states that 'it is difficult to say whether the Absolute is to be regarded as a self or not — that is to say, whether what is called the absolute experience possesses the centrality or focalized unity which is the essential characteristic of a self' (p. 271). On the other hand he asserts (against Spinoza) that intelligence, will and purpose are predicable of God (15); but later he says that the attribution of personality to God is 'the denial of an error (16) rather than a definitely articulated affirmation of ascertained fact' (p. 390).

3. Pringle-Pattison has to admit that he cannot explain how finite selves can be included in God. Yet his chief criticism of Bradley is that the latter fails to explain how the 'apparent' world of finite multiplicity is absorbed into the undifferentiated 'reality' of the Absolute. It seems to me that Pringle-Pattison is here even more vulnerable than Bradley. If

96

it is hard to see how appearances can be created by (and, in turn, merged into) a unitary Absolute, it is harder still to see how mutually exclusive and impermeable selves can be included in and permeated by God. Pringle-Pattison surely here falls into self-contradiction. One can evade the contradiction only by supposing either that God is not a 'self', or that his selfhood differs entirely from its human copies. As we have seen, Pringle-Pattison is agnostic concerning the applicability of selfhood to God. But if we say that God's selfhood differs wholly from ours and is therefore wholly unknowable, we expose ourselves to objections that Pringle-Pattison brings against Spencer (17).

4. There is the question of epistemology. How do we know that God exists and possesses the properties that Pringle-Pattison ascribes (albeit ambiguously) to him? Do we know by the metaphysical act of faith described on pp. 239-42 (18) or by the kind of distinctively religious experience hinted at on p. 252? It is strange that Pringle-Pattison (who fully acknowledges the interdependence of metaphysics and epistemology) does not examine these questions more thoroughly.

5. Pringle-Pattison shows himself remarkably insensitive to the premiss of the cosmological argument. 'It is fruitless', he asserts on p. 174, 'to inquire how there comes to be anything at all . . . we, as philosophers, have not to explain why there should be a universe at all, but to find out what kind of universe it is.' But if the universe is, as it manifestly is, contingent, the question of why it exists is, no less manifestly, the primary one for metaphysical speculation. The only question then is: 'Which is the more satisfactory answer — panentheism or theism?'

6. Pringle-Pattison's would-be reinterpretation of Christianity is a distortion of it. The God of the Bible — the transcendent, personal Creator of the world who redeemed mankind by a unique act of Incarnation and Atonement — is one kind of God; the Hegelian Absolute is another; and nothing but confusion results from an attempt to synthesise or equate them.

(b) Barth

It is widely agreed that, if only in terms of the scale on which he has written and the influence he has exercised, Karl Barth is the greatest theologian since Aquinas. In sheer volume and range his 'Die Kirchliche Dogmatik' constitutes the only parallel to the 'Summa Theologica'. Hence it is inevitable that he should have a section to himself in a survey of modern theology. It is equally inevitable that, in the space at my disposal, I can examine only a fraction of the 'Church Dogmatics'. I shall concentrate on the main elements in chapter 6 (entitled 'The Reality of God') in the first half-volume of volume 2 (19).

Barth's whole theology is determined by the stress that he lays on God's transcendence and incomprehensibility. God is the 'wholly other'. Between him and all his creatures there is 'an infinite qualitative distinction'. We cannot know him as he is in himself — as he exists in his ineffable majesty. Hence Barth vigorously opposes any form of pantheism or panentheism. Hence too he opposes any attempt to comprehend God by metaphysical speculation. Like Kierkegaard, he is to be largely understood in terms of his reaction against Hegelian rationalism.

Yet Barth does not stop here. He denies that it is possible to have even a limited knowledge of God apart from Christian revelation. His repudiation of natural theology is absolute (20). Equally he refuses to allow that non-Christians have ever known God to any extent in non-rational ways (for example, through mystical intuition). 'We cannot be sufficiently eager to insist, nor can it be sufficiently emphasised in the Church, that we know God in Jesus Christ alone, and that in Jesus Christ we know the one true God' (p. 318).

Consequently, there is no 'point of contact' between Christian and non-Christian concepts of God. 'God', Barth writes is his 'Dogmatics in Outline', 'is not to be regarded as a continuation and enrichment of the concepts and ideas which usually constitute religious thought in general about God. The God of the Christian Confession is, in distinction from all gods, not a found or invented God; he is not a fulfilment of what man was in course of seeking and finding' (21).

An interesting example of Barth's restriction of theological truth to Christian revelation occurs on pp. 603-7, where he is discussing the idea of divine 'omnipotence'. We do not, he says, obtain this idea through rational reflection on the world or through any analogical extension of the concept 'power'. Let us look at the Scriptures. There we find that Isaiah and Jeremiah discerned God's omnipotence in his salvation of Israel (p. 603). Even more profoundly, Barth urges, we learn from 1 Corinthians 1:24 that God's power is known in and through the Cross of Christ. 'It is, therefore, the knowledge of Jesus Christ the Crucified which is the knowledge of the omnipotent knowing and willing of God' (p. 607).

Therefore Barth insists that a true understanding of God must start from the doctrine of the Trinity (22). Through the Scriptures God is revealed as a threefold Being, Father, Son and Holy Spirit. If, then, all our knowledge of God is a response to his Word of Revelation, we must consider him in his triunity. This is how Barth puts it on p. 261, with reference to a quotation from Polanus: 'It was certainly right to define the essence of God: *Essentia Dei est ipsa Deitas, qua Deus a se et per se absolute est et existit.* But even in the definition of this *a se et per se* there ought never to have been an abstraction from the Trinity, and that means from the act of divine revelation.'

In a widely read essay written in 1956 Barth, in looking back on his theological career, finds that in the twenties he underestimated what he calls 'the humanity of God' (23). But it is important to realise what he intends by this phrase. In his own words, in the first paragraph of the essay, 'it represents God's existence, intercession, and activity for man, the intercourse God holds with him, and the free grace in which he wills to be and is nothing other than the God of man'. All that Barth means is that in his earlier works he had so far stressed God's 'otherness' that he gave too little emphasis to God's love for, and co-operation with, men. But Barth still holds that God's love and grace are known only through Christ (24). Admittedly on pp. 54-5 his attitude to human culture and morality reaches an unprecedented point

99

of generosity. Yet even here he speaks of man as 'a downright monster'. In any case so far as the nature of God and the means by which we know him are concerned, he does not say anything in this essay that he does not say, with the same balance, and more fully, in the 'Church Dogmatics', to which I now return.

The first thing, Barth says, that we learn from revelation is that God is 'life'. God is, in the Biblical phrase, 'the living God'. Hence 'it was quite right when the older theology described the essence of God as *vita*, and again as *actuositas*, or more simply as *actus*' (p. 263). The living God includes, but also transcends, Nature and Spirit. After noting the frequency with which the Old Testament writers attribute physical features to Yahweh, Barth writes thus: 'As God's thoughts are not our thoughts, as his Spirit is not our spirit, so obviously his eyes are not human eyes, nor his hands human hands. But it does mean that what is said naturally about God is not to be arbitrarily translated into something spiritual. The divine being must be allowed to transcend both spirit and nature, yet also to overlap and comprehend both' (p. 266).

The living God, as pure *actus*, is also self-existent. He alone is 'self-motivated' (p. 271); he alone 'is what he is absolutely by himself, and not by anything else that would confer divinity upon him' (p. 273)' 'Of God we can say only that in the actuality of his being he is its affirmation, that in the actuality of his being his non-being, or his being other than he is, is ontologically and noetically excluded' (p. 307).

Barth's distinctive way of expressing God's *aseitas* is through the concept of 'freedom'. 'By freedom we denote what was called in the theology of the Early Church the *aseitas Dei*' (p. 302). On its negative side God's freedom means 'the absence of limits, restrictions, or conditions'. On its positive side it means 'to be grounded in one's own being, to be determined and moved by oneself' (p. 301). God's freedom, thus understood, constitutes the unique form of his sovereignty.

God's actuality and aseity must determine our understanding of his attributes. God does not merely *have* power; he *is* power (p. 542). Similarly 'his being is itself also his

100

knowledge' (p. 549). I shall recur to Barth's teaching on this point when I consider his account of God's 'perfections'.

Furthermore (as the passages I have quoted imply), God is personal. Against the view that the ascription of personality to God is anthropomorphic, Barth maintains that God is the primary Person: 'Everything outside him is secondary. It exists only on the basis of his gracious creation and providence. And it can be known only by God's Word and revelation. We cannot speak of 'personalising' in reference to God's being, but only in reference to ours. The real person is not man but God. It is not God who is a person by extension, but we' (pp. 271-2).

The essence of God's personality is love:

> No change of theme was involved when we spoke first of God's life and then of God's love, first of his being in act and then of his being as One who loves. It was not as if we knew first and in general of God's life as such and only then provided this generalised subject with its specialised predicate, that is the life and ruling of love. But God's life itself and as such is in all its depths the loving of God, and only in preparation for this insight, only in development of the prior logical assertion that God is an acting Subject, did we linger for a moment to reflect upon God's being in act, which is in no sense act in general but the concrete, specific action of his love (25).

In an important and scholarly excursus (26) Barth maintains that theology took a fatally wrong turn when it chose as its starting-point, not the triune God of love, but God in general. God's personality then became problematical. The infinite Spirit arrived at by philosophical speculation became contrasted with the personal God of the Bible. Hence when philosophers tried to justify the ascription of personality to God they did so on subjective grounds. We speak of the Absolute as personal (they said) because personality is the highest category we know, and because the idea of a personal God satisfies our spiritual aspirations. But this justification does not assure us that God is really (much less that he is

101

essentially) personal. Moreover, it lends immediate support to the view that belief in a personal God is merely a psychological 'projection' (27).

God's love is his motive for creating the world. Yet he does not need the world; for he is self-sufficient in love, as in every other attribute. His love for us is the 'overflowing' of the love with which he loves himself within his triune being. 'Therefore his love for us is his *eternal* love, and our being loved by him is our being taken up into the fellowship of his eternal love, in which he is himself for ever and ever' (p. 280).

By his creative power God is immanent in the world. His immanence is correlative to his transcendence. 'Now the absoluteness of God means that God has the freedom to be present with that which is not God, to communicate himself and unite himself with the other, and the other with himself, in a way which utterly surpasses all that can be effected in regard to reciprocal presence, communion, and fellowship between other beings' (p. 313). God, moreover, indwells creatures in diverse ways according to their characteristics and his intentions for them (pp. 314-16).

Having thus established the basic principles of his theology, Barth deals with God's 'perfections'. Here he is anxious to dissociate himself from the two following positions.

First, there is 'the strict nominalistic thesis as represented by Eunomius in antiquity and William of Occam in the Middle Ages. According to this all individual and distinct statements about the being of God have no other value than that of purely subjective ideas and descriptions (*conceptus, nomina*) to which there is no corresponding reality in God who is pure simplicity' (p. 327). Secondly, according to the traditional view (held by both Aquinas and Calvin), the perfections we ascribe to God really belong to him, but not in the multiple and diverse manner in which our finite minds are forced to conceive them. Yet Barth dismisses this view as 'partial nominalism' (p. 330).

Barth affirms that God 'is in essence not only one, but multiple, individual and diverse' (p. 331). Multiplicity does not contradict unity; for each of God's properties expresses his whole nature. 'Our doctrine therefore means that every

102

individual perfection in God is nothing but God himself and therefore nothing but every other divine perfection. It means equally strictly on the other hand that God himself is nothing other than each one of his perfections in its individuality, and that each individual perfection is identical with every other and with the fulness of them all' (p. 333).

Barth then proceeds to examine the following divine perfections: grace, holiness, mercy, righteousness, patience, wisdom, unity, omnipresence, constancy, omnipotence, eternity and glory. I shall take as examples of his approach the ideas of 'constancy' (or 'immutability') and 'eternity'. I have chosen these because (as we have already seen with reference to both theism and panentheism) they are the most disputable.

Barth begins by affirming God's immutability in these terms: 'There neither is nor can be in him, the one and omnipresent being, any deviation, diminution, or addition, any degeneration or rejuvenation, any alteration or non-identity or discontinuity' (p. 491). But he adds that God is not immobile; for 'the pure *immobile* is death' (p. 494). He goes even further on p. 496 by asserting, with deliberate paradox, that 'there is such a thing as a holy mutability of God', that since he is immanent in finite alteration 'there is something corresponding to that alteration in his own essence', and that 'his constancy consists in the fact that he is always the same in every change'. Hence we must take seriously, not just figuratively, Biblical assertions concerning God's 'repentance' (28).

Barth's treatment of 'eternity' is also paradoxical. He begins, again, by stating the traditional standpoint of Christian theism. On p. 608, having said that 'eternity is not an infinite extension of time', and that 'time can have nothing to do with God', he quotes with approval a typical passage in which St Augustine affirms God's simultaneity. Yet he also says that eternity is temporal. 'Eternity is really beginning, really middle, and really end' (p. 639). He attempts to reconcile these apparently conflicting statements thus: 'God's beginning includes not only his goal or end, but also the whole way to it. In his present there occurs both the beginning and the end. At God's end, his beginning is operative in all its power, and his present is still present' (p. 640).

There are, I suggest, four main ways in which Barth's doctrine of God brings fresh light to bear on Christian theism.

1. Barth consistently unites the idea of God as Being with the idea of him as personal. These two ideas have sometimes been separated (provisionally, if not ultimately) by Christian philosophers and theologians. There are two major examples of the separation among twentieth-century theologians. On the one hand Tillich, after defining God non-symbolically, as Being-itself, fails to clarify the status of the personal symbols through which God is described by Christians. On the other hand, many existentialists have spoken of God *ab initio* as personal, but without seeming to realise that his personality infinitely exceeds ours in its form of being. Barth constantly affirms both truths simultaneously. He never separates belief in God as the incomprehensible mystery of unconditioned Being from belief in him as the personal Father whose love and grace are uniquely revealed in Jesus of Nazareth. God, for Barth, could be defined as either personally infinite or infinitely personal.

2. Equally, Barth maintains a true balance between the ideas of transcendence and immanence. He is chiefly known, understandably, for his teaching on God's transcendence. Yet we must not forget that he attaches equal weight to God's immanence in, not only the order of grace, but also the order of creation. The Creator, he affirms, is nearer to his creatures than they can ever be to each other. Also, he adds, God's mode of presence is perfectly adapted to the nature of each created entity and to his loving purpose for it.

3. Barth is also to be commended for his reconciliation of belief in God's creative love with belief in God's *aseitas* (or self-sufficiency). In accordance with his determination to interpret divine Being from the outset through the personal categories of revelation, he affirms that God's self-sufficiency takes the form of his triune love. God's act in creating the world is the 'overflowing' of his love. Barth here does full justice both to the Bible and to the Platonic insight that

104

God's goodness is essentially self-diffusing.

4. Although Barth holds that we can know God only through Christian revelation, he makes a sustained attempt to articulate this knowledge in rational terms. He is anti-rationalist in so far as he rejects all forms of rational (or natural) theology. But he firmly believes that God's revelation can be rationally discussed (29). And his discussion is immensely thorough. He argues rigorously; he quotes an impressive array of both Protestant and Catholic sources; and he obviously seeks (even if he does not always achieve) consistency.

Barth has been criticised (often, one suspects, by those who have not read him) for being unbalanced and irrational. In fact he achieves a large degree of balance and rationality. Yet the sad thing is that, in spite of his great learning and outstanding gifts, he is prevented by his presuppositions from achieving the maximum degree. And so I come, reluctantly, to my objections.

1. Barth exaggerates the differences between himself and the scholastics (especially Aquinas). Thus, although Aquinas began his natural theology by defining God, non-personally, as 'He Who Is' (or self-existent Being), he also held that God's spiritual (and so personal) attributes could be deduced from this definition. Again, Barth's affirmation of the manner in which these attributes coinhere is fully congruous with Aquinas's concept of divine simplicity. Finally, Barth makes many statements that imply the Thomist doctrine of analogy (30).

2. It may well be doubted whether 'freedom' can discharge the theistic function that Barth claims for it. Obviously God is 'free' in the sense that he is not subject to any external conditions. But to say that he is free from such conditions is to say that he is self-existent (or that he exists *a se*). Barth admits all this. My only point is that 'freedom' cannot indicate the uniqueness of God unless (on Barth's own admission) it is further qualified in terms of being. Why, then, does Barth persist in regarding 'freedom' as a theistically self-sufficient notion? Only, I think, because he is prejudiced against ontology in general and Thomist ontology

105

in particular.

3. Barth's view of God as one who is characterised by 'Nature' as well as 'Spirit' is obscure. On the one hand he affirms the incorporeality of God. On the other hand he holds that there are elements in God's being that correspond to our physical organs. The idea of such a correspondence is very hard (in my opinion impossible) to entertain. The only view that seems to me to make any kind of sense is that (as Thomists maintain), although spiritual attributes are predicable of God according to an analogy of proportionality, material attributes can be predicated of him only as metaphors. Barth's obscurity here is due, I think, to two factors: his rejection of the idea of *analogia entis* ('analogy of being'), and his failure to adopt a sufficiently critical attitude to the Bible. I shall consider these factors in my next two criticisms.

4. Barth does not distinguish clearly enough between the order of being and the order of knowing. Let us take his key-concept of personality. He is right to insist that in the order of being God is (as he must be if he is the Creator) primary; he is 'the father from whom every family in heaven and on earth is named' (31). But in the order of knowing human personality is primary. The only form of personality that we immediately and positively know is our own. Hence it is only in terms of our own personality that we can speak of its divine archetype. And we cannot thus speak unless there is an analogy of being between God and us (32).

5. Although Barth formally repudiates Biblical fundamentalism, there are strong traces of it in his thought. Thus he is determined to give some (though an unspecified) ground in God's nature for every personal image that is theistically used in the Bible. I have already commented on the difficulty involved in his attribution of physical (or 'natural') terms to the incorporeal God. His uncritical acceptance of the Old Testament's ascription of 'repentance' to God leads him to describe God paradoxically as both mutable and immutable. Similarly his acceptance of the Biblical identification of eternity with unending time compels him to speak of God as both timeless and temporal. But are these strictly paradoxes (that is, statements which appear to be, but in fact are not,

106

contrary to reason)? Are they not instances of sheer self-contradiction?

6. Barth's view that there is no knowledge of God apart from Christian revelation is the aspect of his thought that has been most fiercely debated. And the debate has often engendered more heat than light. It seems to me that three simple things need to be said from the standpoint of Christian orthodoxy. First, Christianity (being based on the unique and once-for-all event of the Incarnation) differs, not only in degree, but also in kind from all other religious systems. Secondly, a *saving* knowledge of God can occur only through Christ (33). But, thirdly, even if these two tenets are true, they do not entail the view that all non-Christian concepts of God are totally false. On the contrary, it is an easily verifiable and incontrovertible fact that there are major resemblances to the Christian concept of God in a wide variety of non-Christian religions — in (to give only three examples that immediately occur to me) the Aeschylean vision of Zeus, Plotinus's teaching on the ineffably transcendent One, and the devotion to a personal Lord that characterises Indian *bhakti*-religion.

There are two reasons why Barth refuses to allow any measure of truth to non-Christian forms of theology. First, he assumes that unless non-Christians can *prove* God's existence and have a *full* knowledge of him they must be totally idolatrous. But it is possible to hold that non-Christians possess a (logically) non-probative and partial knowledge of God. Secondly, Barth assumes that the doctrine of Original Sin entails a total ignorance of God on the part of non-Christians. But all the Doctrine entails is that apart from Christ no man can have a *perfect* knowledge of God's nature or render *perfect* obedience to God's will.

(c) Brunner

Brunner is always closely associated with Barth in surveys of twentieth-century thought. The association is valid in so far as both wrote large-scale works of dogmatic theology in which they sought to reaffirm the fullness of Biblical revelation in the face of philosophical rationalism and theological liberalism. I shall first summarise and comment on Brunner's doctrine of God. I shall then indicate the main points of comparison and contrast between him and Barth (34).

Brunner begins by defining the nature and scope of Christian dogmatics. The ultimate source and object of Christian revelation is Christ himself; and the primary witness to Christ is contained in the New Testament, which is thus the norm of Christian belief and practice. The creeds and confessions of the Church, though indispensable, are subordinate to the Scriptures. The task of the dogmatic theologian is to interpret revelation in the light of the New Testament and the credal statements that are based on it. At the same time the theologian must not be enslaved by these sources. He must 'distinguish within the Scriptures that which is binding and valid from that which is conditioned by human and contemporary circumstances' (p. 81). Also 'it is not for us to reproduce the doctrine of Zwingli or of Calvin, but to seek the truth, even if this may lead us to speak *against* Zwingli and Calvin, and *for* Luther, or even against the doctrine of the Reformers as a whole' (p. 82).

The main theses of the book are as follows. God is a personal mystery whom we know through his self-revelation in Christ. 'God is not an 'object' which man can manipulate by his own reasoning; he is a Mystery dwelling in the depths of 'inaccesible Light' ' (p. 117). This divine mystery is also personal. He is the supreme Subject, the absolute 'I' whom his human creatures can address as 'Thou'. But we do not know the personal mystery of God through speculation on his hidden essence; we know him through those media (attested by the Scriptures) by which he has chosen to disclose himself. These basic axioms are stated in the opening chapters of part 1 on 'The Name of God', 'God the Lord' and 'The Holy' (where Brunner pays high tribute to Otto). In the course of these chapters Brunner makes three particular points that merit notice.

(a) Belief in the transcendence — the mystery and holiness — of God is a distinctive element in the Old Testament. 'The whole conflict between Yahweh and the Baalim of the Near East raged round this essential Transcendence of God; the conflict raged between the God who is the 'Wholly Other' and the nature-gods, who were only hypostasized forces of Nature. That is why the commandment forbidding the worship of graven images was of such decisive significance' (p. 159).

(b) In revealing his nature God simultaneously conceals it in the media of his revelation. Quoting from Luther, Brunner writes thus: 'The revelation of God, from the standpoint of his absolute, non-revealed *'majestas'*, is a gracious veiling of that devastating Majesty. In this connection we must understand the new pair of opposites, *Deus nudus, Deus velatus*. The *Deus nudus* is that naked Majesty, the sight of whom is intolerable for the sinful creature, 'God merely and apart from Christ'. Over against this God the sinner 'is without protection or shade in the blazing sun'. It is only the gracious veiling of this terrible Majesty in the human Person of the Redeemer 'which protects us from the heat which comes from the contemplation of the Divine Majesty' ' (p. 171).

(c) To the objection that the idea of a personal God is anthropomorphic Brunner replies as follows: 'The question whether the application of the idea of 'person' to God is an anthropomorphism, receives a remarkable answer from the standpoint of the Biblical idea of God. The question is not whether *God* is personality, but whether *man* is. It is not the personal being of God which is 'anthropomorphic', but, conversely, the personal being of man is a 'theomorphism'. God alone is truly Person; man is only person in a symbolic way, as a reflection of God, as the *Imago Dei*' (p. 140).

Brunner then proceeds to amplify this basic account of the divine nature. The God who is holy is also loving. Brunner bases his description of God's love on Nygren's contrast between *eros* and *agape*. Platonic *eros* is love for what is intrinsically lovable; and it implies a need for the object loved. 'The Love of God, the *Agape* of the New Testament, is quite different. It does not seek value, but it creates value or gives value; it does not desire to get but to give; it is not 'attracted' by some lovable quality, but it is poured out on

109

those who are worthless and degraded' (p. 186). And because God has no need of his creatures, his love is unique in its excellence and purity. 'Only the God who in himself possesses all perfection, who is perfectly self-sufficient and needs no other, can love in freedom, can love unfathomably' (p. 189).

Brunner sees the doctrine of the Trinity as providing the ground for his concept of divine love. 'God is not merely the loving One in his relation to us. He 'is love'. This highest and most daring word of the New Testament, and of human speech as a whole, is only possible if the love of God is really 'before the foundation of the world', if therefore God is in himself the One who loves' (p. 228). Brunner further claims that the trinitarian belief in God as a being whose inner life is one of mutual love is necessary for the affirmation that God is personal 'in himself', and not only in his relation to the world:

> If God were not in himself Love, but only became so through his relation to the world, then only in relation to the world would he be personal; in himself he would be impersonal. The personal being of Jesus Christ is not merely a πρόσωπον of God, a personal theophany, but the personal being of Jesus Christ is the personal Being of God himself. From all eternity, before there was any world at all, God is the One who speaks and loves; the Word does not arise first of all as a means of communication to the world; from all eternity it is an integral part of the nature of God. Only when we have thus traced the Biblical idea of God back to its ultimate source can we finally eliminate that Hegelian idea of the God who 'becomes personal' within the sphere of history. Yet all this is already implicit in the simple statement of faith: God, the Father of our Lord Jesus Christ (35).

In the remaining chapters of the book Brunner states his views on the other divine attributes. God is almighty (within the self-imposed limits required by the reality of human freedom) (36); he is omnipresent and omniscient; he is eternal

110

in the sense that he is sovereign over the temporal order he has created; he is absolutely righteous and wise in all his acts. In discussing these attributes Brunner takes account of both Catholic and Protestant formulations; but he tests both by the ultimate criterion, or norm, of the Scriptures.

Although Brunner's terminology and emphases may seem strange and even uncongenial to Christians who do not belong to his theological tradition, there can be no doubt that he states forcefully, and with manifest sincerity, the substance of those dogmatic affirmations that have been made by orthodox Catholics and Protestants alike. His book is to be specially welcomed for integrating the ideas of transcendence, personality, self-sufficiency and love. Furthermore, although he is faithful to the central teaching of the Reformers he is not enslaved by their categories of thought, and does not fear to depart from them when such a departure is demanded by the Scriptures.

There is, however, one pervasive characteristic of the book which is highly disputable. This is its anti-philosophical tendency. Brunner constantly opposes the personal, concrete, 'subjective' language of the Bible to the impersonal, abstract, 'objective' language of philosophy in general and Greek philosophy in particular. 'The relation of the 'God' of Plato or of Aristotle with the God of the Biblical revelation is that of Either—Or. The same may be said of every other idea of God which has been attained purely by philosophical speculation' (p. 136). Brunner amplifies this judgement thus on p. 139: 'The God with whom we have to do in faith, is not a Being who has been discussed or 'conceived' (by man); he is not an *Ens*, a 'substance', like the Godhead of metaphysical speculation; he is not an object of thought — even though in a sublimated and abstract form — but the Subject who as 'I' addresses us as 'thou'. God is the personality who speaks, acts, disclosing to us himself and his will.'

Admittedly there is some truth in the contrasts that Brunner affirms. Many concepts of God in non-Christian systems of philosophy have fallen far short of the fully personal concept found in the Bible. Again, Christian theologians themselves need constantly to be on their guard lest

111

they obscure God's personal reality by their abstract formulations or suggest that the latter enable us to comprehend him 'as he is'. Lastly, the theologian must always remember that distinctively Christian knowledge is obtained, not by metaphysical thought, but by a response to God's self-revelation. Nevertheless, it seems to me that the *absolute* contrast (the *unqualified* Either—Or) that Brunner posits between metaphysics and revelation is invalid for the following reasons.

1. Brunner's attitude to philosophers and philosophy is inconsistent. It does not always take the rigid form I have just illustrated. Thus after a pejorative reference to Aristotle he writes as follows of Stoicism: 'On the other hand, the relation between the Christian idea of God and that of Stoic popular philosophy seems much closer — Cicero, Epictetus, Seneca, Marcus Aurelius. But, on the one hand, it is very questionable to what extent we can here speak of philosophical thought at all; and on the other hand, we must not forget that all these thinkers lived at a time when the Hebrew idea of God was already at work, like leaven, in contemporary thought' (p. 153).

This passage is highly tendentious. The Greeks and Romans whom Brunner names are universally regarded as philosophers; and there is not the slightest evidence that they were subject to Hebrew influence. Moreover, if we discern elements of theistic truth in Stoicism we must also acknowledge it in Platonism and Hinduism.

Again, Brunner explicitly endorses many of the metaphysical terms through which the scholastics described God. Thus he admits on pp. 142-5 that in order to clarify the Biblical picture of God it is permissible to use the terms 'the Absolute', *ens a se* (or *aseitas*), and *actus purus*. He even says that the idea of aseity is 'indispensable'. Yet on p. 120 he accuses the Greek Fathers of a 'great mistake' in translating the divine name, revealed in Exodus, as 'He Who Is'. But if we take this translation (as Aquinas took it), not as a substitute for, but as a metaphysical analysis of, the personal terms that the Bible applies to Yahweh, it is no less justified than the terms that Brunner himself accepts. Indeed 'aseity'

112

and 'necessity' (in the absolute and factual sense under consideration) are identical.

2. In opposing the 'subjective' nature of revelation to the 'objective' nature of metaphysics Brunner fails to distinguish between different senses of 'object'. Because I think 'about' God and make 'objective' statements about him, it does not follow that I convert him into an object (= impersonal 'thing'). Such thought and such statements are inevitable ingredients in any response to God's personal self-revelation. *Pace* Brunner's assertions on p. 139 (which I quoted earlier) the God of the Bible *is* (even within the Bible itself) a Being who is 'conceived' and 'discussed'; he *is* 'an object of thought'. If he were not an object of thought the Biblical writers could not have made any statements about him. *A fortiori* if he were not such an object Brunner (*qua* dogmatic theologian) could not say of him that he is 'the Personality who speaks, acts, disclosing to us his will'.

3. Because Brunner is so half-hearted in his acceptance of metaphysical analysis, and because he persists in opposing philosophy to the Scriptures, he fails to see that his own dogmatic statements call for further elucidation and that the latter is bound to involve the use of philosophical categories. This is especially evident in his treatment of God's eternity and immutability.

On the one hand Brunner affirms that God is changeless: 'A God who is constantly changing is not a God whom we can worship; he is a mythological being for whom we can only feel sorry' (p. 269). On the other hand Brunner has said on the previous page that God changes through being affected by his human creatures: 'God 'reacts' to the acts of man, and in that he 'reacts' he changes.' Like Barth, Brunner makes no attempt to harmonise his conflicting statements. At least it can be said on behalf of Hartshorne that he *tries* to give a metaphysical account of the dipolarity that he posits in the Godhead.

Brunner's account of divine eternity is similarly incomplete. He criticises Cullmann's 'Christ and Time' on the ground that 'it retains the unresolved contradiction between the thought that God is Lord of time, and that he himself has a share in

113

the temporal form' (p. 267). Yet he deliberately confines himself to stating that 'the idea of eternity means the sovereignty of God over Time which he has created' (p. 271). This statement fails to settle the question that Brunner himself raises with regard to Cullmann. Either God is temporal or he is timeless. The assertion (true so far as it goes) that God is Lord of our temporal world does not exempt us from the necessity of choosing between these alternatives.

The similarities between Brunner and Barth are obvious. Both regard the Scriptures as the source and norm of revelation; both emphasise God's transcendence and personality; both affirm that the revealed God is simultaneously the hidden God; both interpret God's *aseitas* and sovereignty through the concept of 'freedom'; both appeal to the doctrine of the Trinity as justification of the paradoxical claim that God creates, out of love, a world which he does not need. It is therefore not surprising that these theologians are so often classed together.

However, there are also differences between the two. On the one hand, Brunner admits that non-Christians possess *some* knowledge of God, and that this constitutes a 'point of contact' for grace; but Barth continues to deny any kind of natural theology or, therefore, anything in natural religion to which the Gospel can appeal (37). On the other hand, Brunner is more emphatic in the contrast he continually — indeed, tediously — draws between subject and object, 'I' and 'It', encounter and speculation. Barth, of course affirms that all our knowledge of God is derived from Christian revelation; but he lays greater stress on the necessity for rational understanding of the God who is thus revealed. Hence his theology is more thorough, more speculative and more abstract.

Yet when Barth and Brunner are viewed in the light of Christian theism as a whole, their similarities are more striking than their differences. Their allegiance to the Protestant tradition was both liberating and restricting. It was liberating in so far as it enabled them to discern afresh (when such discernment was greatly needed) the truths of God's transcendence, personality and love. It was restricting in so far as it rendered them, partly or wholly, insensitive to the testimony borne to these truths by natural theology and non-Christian religions.

(d) Radhakrishnan

I have chosen Radhakrishnan for two reasons. First, he is the most distinguished and influential Indian thinker of his generation. Secondly, he has aimed at uniting the religious insights of the Hindu East and the Christian West. Although I think (and hope to show) that he achieves union at the expense of ignoring differences, I wish to express my admiration for the breadth, sensitivity and clarity of his writings. From the latter I have chosen 'The Hindu View of Life' (38) and 'Recovery of Faith' (39).

In 'The Hindu View of Life' Radhakrishnan insists that Hinduism is a non-dogmatic religion: 'It did not regard it as its mission to convert humanity to any one opinion. For what counts is conduct and not belief' (p. 38). Consequently 'the theist and the atheist, the sceptic and the agnostic, may all be Hindus if they accept the Hindu system of culture and life' (p. 77). In its intellectual tolerance Hinduism, so Radhakrishnan claims, shows its superiority to Semitic religions.

Nevertheless, Radhakrishnan affirms that all Hindus believe in the existence of a supreme Spirit. 'The Hindu never doubted the reality of one supreme universal spirit, however much the descriptions of it may fall short of its nature' (p. 25). Two questions now arise. What is the nature of this Spirit? What is its (or his) relation to the world? The attempt to answer these questions will take us to the heart of Radhakrishnan's thought.

First, then, what is the nature of the supreme Spirit (or God)? More particularly, is God personal or non-personal? Radhakrishnan often states that God *per se* — God in his essence — is supra-personal. Thus on pp. 19-20 he distinguishes between a personal God and 'the Supreme'. More explicitly he grades concepts of God thus on p. 32:

115

Hinduism insists on our working steadily upwards and improving our knowledge of God. The worshippers of the Absolute are the highest in rank; second to them are the worshippers of the personal God; then come the worshippers of the incarnations like Rama, Krishna, Buddha; below them are those who worship ancestors, deities and sages, and lowest of all are the worshippers of the petty forces and spirits (40).

On this view Christianity, being based on faith in the Incarnation of a personal God, is a second-class religion. Hence Radhakrishnan writes as follows on p. 46: 'Suppose a Christian approaches a Hindu teacher for spiritual guidance, he would not ask his Christian pupil to discard his allegiance to Christ, but would tell him that his idea of Christ was not adequate and would lead him to a knowledge of the real Christ, the incorporate Supreme.'

Radhakrishnan proceeds to affirm that belief in a suprapersonal Absolute is present in all religions, and is the ground of their hidden unity. He gives two reasons for this affirmation.

First, he says, the *via negativa* is universal. 'The *neti* of Yajnavalkya reminds us of the *nescio* of Bernard, of 'the dim silence where all lovers lose themselves' of Ruysbroeck, of the negative descriptions of Dionysius the Areopagite, Eckhart and Boehme' (p. 26).

Secondly (as the preceding quotation indicates), Radhakrishnan points to (as he sees it) the universal testimony of mysticism to the supra-personal character of God. Thus he says on p. 30 that 'the personal category is transcended in the highest experiences of the Christian mystics'. On p. 34 he quotes Evelyn Underhill for the view that there is no difference between the Brahmin, the Sufi or Christian mystics at their best; and on p. 60 he contrasts the spiritual unity of the mystics with the intellectual exclusiveness of dogmatic theologians.

If God is essentially supra-personal, how can we justify the application of personal terms to him? We can justify it, so Radhakrishnan asserts (in company with many other religious thinkers), on the ground that 'the personal' is the highest

116

category that we know within finite experience:

> The religious seer needs the help of the imagination to
> express his vision. 'Without a parable spake he not unto
> them.' The highest category we can use is that of self-
> conscious personality. We are persons, 'purusas', and God
> is perfect personality (*uttamapurusa*). If we analyse the
> concept of personality we find that it includes cognition,
> emotion, and will, and God is viewed as the supreme
> knower, the great lover, and the perfect will, Brahama,
> Visnu, Siva (41).

What, then, is the metaphysical status of the personal
qualities that we predicate of God? Radhakrishnan gives two
differing answers on pp. 29-31. On the one hand he affirms
that personal terms 'do not tell us about what God is in
himself but only what he is to us'. On the other hand he says
that God actually expresses himself in a personal mode. 'The
same God expresses itself at one stage as power, at another
as personality, at a third as all-comprehensive spirit, just as
the same forces which put forth the green leaves also cause
the crimson flowers to grow.'

Yet at other times Radhakrishnan speaks as if God were
ultimately — in his inmost being — personal. Thus on pp.
18-19 he refers, without qualification, to God's 'wisdom',
'love' and 'providence'. Again, on p. 50 he asserts that
religious bigotry 'is inconsistent with an all-loving God'. Later
on he emphasises God's mercy, justice and forgiveness. Thus,
in the course of discussing Karma he writes (in words that
recall St Paul's doctrine of Justification): 'forgiveness is not a
mitigation of God's justice but only an expression of it' (p.
74).

The second question raised by Radhakrishnan concerns the
relationship between God and the world. When he is thinking
theistically (as in the passages quoted in the preceding paragraph), he interprets this relationship in terms of creation.
But his final interpretation is panentheistic. Although God
transcends the world he includes it in his being. The world is
the self-expression of his nature and, therefore, divine. In

order to distinguish his theology from pure pantheism, Radhakrishnan writes that 'the world is in God, and not God in the world' (p. 71). However, in the next paragraph he asserts that on account of God's immanence (which he describes through the metaphor of 'the divine spark') 'the worst of the world cannot be dismissed as completely undivine'. Yet although he commits himself so far to panentheism he says that the relation between God and the world is a 'mystery' before which the human mind must remain 'agnostic' (42).

In 'Recovery of Faith' Radhakrishnan expands some of the statements that he made nearly thirty years earlier in 'The Hindu View of Life'. He states that the existence and order of the world demand an explanation in terms of Absolute Being. He then makes two distinctive assertions concerning this Being. First, it is beyond existence:

> Being denotes pure affirmation to the exclusion of every possible negation. It is absolute self-absorbed Being, the one Supreme Identity beyond existence and non-existence, the universal reality. When Moses asked God, after the latter had sent him to Egypt to save his brethren: 'If they should say to me, what is his name? What shall I say to them?' God replied to him: 'You will tell them, I am who I am.' (43).

Secondly, God's being is related to, and includes, non-being:

> The process of the universe is a perpetual overcoming of non-being by Being. Being therefore includes non-being within itself. In the universe, Being affirms itself and overcomes its own non-being. When it is said that God has power, it means that Being will overcome the resistance of non-being. It affirms itself against non-being (44).

Radhakrishnan proceeds to affirm that God is essentially supra-personal, and that his supra-personal character is recognised in all religions. On the page from which I have just quoted we are told that 'the personal God is the first determination from which flow all other determinations'. This statement recalls the thesis, propounded in 'The Hindu View of Life', that personality is one of the modes through which the Absolute 'expresses' itself. On p. 111 the inferior status of personal theism is affirmed in the judgement that 'in the 'Bhagavadgita', contemplation of the Supreme is *mixed up with* devotion to the Absolute as God' (45). Finally, all religions, in their inmost reality, testify to a supra-personal Absolute. 'Throughout the history of Indian religions, Hinduism and Buddhism, Jainism and Sikhism, Christianity and Islam, the stress is more on the renewal of life, the attainment of the transcendental consciousness, than on the worship of a personal God' (p. 113).

Radhakrishnan also states that the non-personal and the personal are two 'sides' of the same Reality. 'When we stress the creative side, the supreme Godhead or the Absolute Brahman is called God. Brahman and Isvara, Godhead and God are one. Brahman refers to infinite being and possibility, and Isvara to creative freedom' (p. 89). But on p. 155 he affirms that different descriptions of God merely reflect different human viewpoints:

The symbols and dogmas are not definitive. Eastern forms of religion hold that differences of interpretation do not affect the one universal truth any more than the differences of colours affect the uncoloured light which is transmitted. Western forms of religion are inclined to hold that one definition is final and absolute and others are false. In India, each definition represents a *darsana* or a viewpoint. There are many ways of viewing one experience. The different *darsanas* are different viewpoints which are not necessarily incompatible. They are pointers on the way to spiritual realisation.

Yet Radhakrishnan's final view is monistic. This emerges clearly in his account of religious intuition. He stresses that belief in God is not mere assent to dogma, still less the entertaining of a hypothesis; it is a direct experience of super-

119

natural reality; it is 'a touching and tasting of the object of knowledge', 'the immediate awareness of Being itself' (p. 105). But on p. 107 this awareness is interpreted in terms of an ontological identity between the knower and the known. The goal of religious experience is the realisation in immediate feeling of the non-dualistic axiom 'That art Thou'. 'The seers of all religions are agreed that there is something in the human soul which is related to the Absolute, which *is* the Absolute' (46).

Radhakrishnan proceeds to interpret the Christian doctrine of the Incarnation in the light of Hindu monism. 'The incarnation', he writes on p. 126, 'is not an historical event which occurred two thousand years ago. It is an event which is renewed in the life of everyone who is on the way to the fulfilment of his destiny.' He offers the same reinterpretation on p. 179. 'God-men are the precursors of the truly human. What is possible for a Gautama or a Jesus is possible for every human being. The nature of man receives its fulfilment in them. In us, ordinary human beings, God-consciousness is darkened, enfeebled, imperfectly developed. In Jesus it is absolutely powerful; the image of God is in full radiance.'

In the mystic's awareness of his spiritual identity with the supra-personal Absolute Radhakrishnan finds 'the transcendent unity of religions' (p. 188). Differences of dogma are irrelevant. 'If we leave aside the secondary interpretations, we find that the seers make practically the same report about the nature of Absolute Reality' (p. 155). Radhakrishnan sums up his book as follows: 'The religion outlined in these pages may be called the sanatana dharma, the eternal religion. It is not to be identified with any particular religion, for it is the religion which transcends race and creed and yet informs all races and creeds' (p. 204).

Radhakrishnan's 'eternal religion' is closely parallel to Aldous Huxley's 'perennial philosophy' (47). By the latter Huxley means the view that God is a supra-personal Absolute to which each human soul is akin or with which it is identical. Thus on p. 8 he writes that 'this teaching is expressed most succinctly in the Sanskrit formula *tat tvam asi* (That art thou); the Atman, or immanent eternal Self, is one with Brahman, the Absolute Principle of all existence; and the last end of every human being is to discover the fact for himself'. Again, on p. 48 he asserts that the spiritual element in man 'is akin to, or even identical with, the divine Spirit that is the Ground of all being'. On p. 71 he states the same monistic point through the metaphor of emanation. 'Every individual being', he says, 'may be thought of as a point where a ray of the primordial Godhead meets one of the differentiated creaturely emanations of that same Godhead's creative energy.'

Huxley usually insists (as I have just indicated) that God 'in himself' is supra-personal. Thus he quotes Sankara approvingly for the view that 'Brahman has neither name nor form' (p. 12) (48). He himself describes the Absolute as the 'God-without-form' and as 'attributeless' (p. 29). Later he affirms that 'God is not a what; he is a that', and that 'the Ground can be denoted as being *there*, but not defined as having qualities' (p. 44).

Like Radhakrishnan, Huxley speaks of personality as an 'aspect' and inferior 'manifestation' of the Absolute. 'The Absolute Ground of all existence has a personal aspect. The activity of Brahman is Isvara, and Isvara is further manifested in the Hindu Trinity and, at a more distant remove, in the other deities or angels of the Indian pantheon' (p. 29). Huxley also resembles Radhakrishnan in denying the uniqueness of God's incarnation in Christ (49); for according to monism God is incarnate in every human soul.

However, Huxley (again like Radhakrishnan) sometimes comes close to the theistic view that God is ultimately, throughout his being, personal. Thus on p. 39 he writes:

The attributeless Godhead of Vedanta, of Mahayana Buddhism, of Christian and Sufi mysticism is the Ground of all the qualities possessed by the personal God. 'God is not good, I am good', says Eckhart. What he really meant was, 'I am just humanly good; God is supereminently good; the Godhead *is* and his 'isness' (*istigheit*, in Eckhart's German) contains goodness, love, wisdom and all the rest in their essence.' In consequence, the Godhead is never, for

121

the exponent of the Perennial Philosophy, the mere Absolute of academic metaphysics, but something more purely perfect, more reverently to be adored than even the personal God or his human incarnation.

In this passage Huxley seems to be saying (in company with classical theists) that God possesses all personal attributes *eminentiori modo*; that his possession of them constitutes his perfection; and that this personal perfection makes him supremely worshipful. Yet Huxley's dominant view is that the Godhead is qualityless, and so *wholly* supra-personal (not merely, as Christian theists would agree, personal in a manner that is beyond our comprehension).

Huxley, however, was not (and did not claim to be) a philosopher. And so I return to Radhakrishnan. It is neces-sary to distinguish between three elements in his thought: his claims for religious intuition, his pleas for mutual religious tolerance and understanding, and his interpretation of the Supernatural. The first and second of these elements are, in my view, admirable. I wholly agree that God is known by a spiritual intuition. And I assume that all my readers will endorse Radhakrishnan's condemnation of religious bigotry.

Yet Radhakrishnan's theology is exposed to the following major criticisms.

1. Radhakrishnan's defence of Hinduism is based on a self-contradiction. On the one hand he praises Hinduism for being non-dogmatic; but on the other hand he says that all Hindus believe in the existence of a supreme Spirit (which, moreover, he defines in pantheistic and panentheistic terms). He fails to see that a completely non-dogmatic religion is impossible (50).

2. Impersonal monism is incompatible with theism. The same X cannot be both qualityless and qualified, both identical with the world (or at any rate with human souls) and the Creator of the world *ex nihilo*. Radhakrishnan's attempts to escape from this dilemma are unconvincing. If (as he sometimes says) the Absolute 'expresses' itself in a personal form, it cannot be entirely non-personal; for it must be characterised by the form that it assumes. But if (as he

says at other times) personal descriptions of God merely represent our subjective viewpoint, we have no guarantee that they have *any* objective reference. Furthermore Radhakrishnan himself often implies that God is ultimately personal.

One could ask two further questions concerning the first (the objective) interpretation of personal theistic terms. First, is not the idea of a wholly supra-personal, qualityless Absolute meaningless? How can we distinguish it from the idea of, simply, 'nothing'? Secondly, how could an impersonal Absolute assume personal properties? The only answer is the one given by Huxley — that it already contains them 'supereminently'. But to give this answer is to endorse the classical theist's view that the Godhead is, essentially and throughout its being, both infinite and personal.

3. Radhakrishnan's equation of impersonal monism with the 'eternal religion' (like Huxley's equation of it with the 'perennial philosophy') is unacceptable. Personal theism is as widespread, even in the East, as impersonal monism (51). To assert that the one form of religious philosophy is more lasting or universal than the other is to commit a sheer error of fact. Both Radhakrishnan and Huxley can make the assertion credible only by initially reducing theism to an inferior status and by reinterpreting (and so distorting) Christian doctrines (especially the doctrine of the Incarnation).

4. It is very hard to understand Radhakrishnan's assertion that the Absolute is 'beyond existence and non-existence'. Certainly the Absolute transcends finite forms of existence; it does not exist as one being among others. But either it does or it does not exist *per se* in a manner appropriate to its nature. Correspondingly, either it is or it is not a mere notion — a mere *ens rationis*. I shall develop this criticism later with reference to Tillich. Meanwhile I shall simply add that in classical theism the verses from Exodus that Radhakrishnan quotes have been taken to signify the identity of existence and essence in God.

5. It is even harder to understand Radhakrishnan's affirmation (which can also be paralleled in Tillich's theology) that

123

the Absolute (*qua* pure Being) includes and overcomes non-being. If 'non-being' means sheer non-existence (τὸ οὐκ ὄν) it cannot be overcome or included. If it means a formless potentiality of being (τὸ μὴ ὄν), I can only repeat that I find this idea meaningless. Moreover, if we say that this potentiality exists outside God as something he must 'overcome' we posit a dualism that is the logical opposite to monism; but if we say that God 'includes' this potentiality we deprive him of the *aseitas* which Radhakrishnan ascribes to him.

6. Radhakrishnan assumes that religious intuition must take a monistic form. But theists claim to intuit a personal God who is totally distinct from the world. If, then, a supernatural Reality exists, which of these 'intuitions' is veridical? Radhakrishnan, in spite of his immense learning and sensitivity, is prevented by his untenable syncretism from answering this question.

(e) Tillich

It would, I think, be true to say that next to Barth and Bultmann Paul Tillich is the most influential (or at any rate the most discussed) of twentieth-century theologians. It is for this reason that I have included him in this survey. I shall add a few words on J. A. T. Robinson's 'Honest to God', which is (as Robinson himself admits) dependent on Tillich's theology.

Tillich has four terms for the Supreme Being: Being (or Being-itself), Ground (or Ground of being), God, and Object of 'ultimate concern'. I shall discuss the senses he attaches to these terms in the first volume of his 'Systematic Theology' (52).

1. *Being-itself.* Tillich claims that both religion and philosophical theology rest on belief in Being-itself — that is, absolute or unconditioned Being in which all finite beings participate and from which they are derived. In order to stress the supremacy and qualitative uniqueness of Being-itself Tillich denies that we can even call it (as both theists

124

and monists have called their versions of the Absolute) 'infinite'. 'Being-itself is not infinity; it is that which lies beyond the polarity of finitude and infinite self-transcendence' (p. 212).

Tillich amplifies this affirmation of pure, unconditioned Being through the other three terms.

2. *Ground (or Ground of being)*. Being-itself is the Ground of all finite beings. This Ground is implicit in our rational attempts to understand the world. 'The depth of reason is the expression of something that is not reason but which precedes reason and is manifest through it' (p. 88). This 'something' can be described in many ways. 'It could be called the 'substance' which appears in the rational structure, or 'being-itself' which is manifest in the *logos* of being, or the 'ground' which is creative in every rational creation, or the 'abyss' which cannot be exhausted by any creation' (ibid.). Yet although being-itself is the ground of all rational processes, it cannot be apprehended without an act of 'ecstasy' in which the reason transcends its normal functions (53).

Tillich does not go far in defining the nature of this 'Ground'. On p. 173 he writes of it thus: 'It oscillates between cause and substance and transcends both of them. It indicates that the ground of revelation is neither a cause which keeps itself at a distance from the revelatory effect nor a substance which effuses itself into the effect, but rather the mystery which appears in revelation and which remains a mystery in its appearance.' In the next sentence he says that the religious equivalent to 'Ground of being' (and so to 'Being-itself') is 'God'. Let us therefore see whether he describes 'God' more positively.

3. *God*. Tillich sometimes describes God in terms that would satisfy a classical theist. 'Things and events', he writes on p. 217, 'have no aseity. This is characteristic only of God.' Again, he affirms that God is personal in so far as he calls God 'Spirit' (p. 276), constantly speaks of him through personal categories, and claims that only a personal God can be the Object of man's 'ultimate concern' (p. 247).

However, there are many non-theistic elements in Tillich's

theology. To begin with, he will not allow that 'existence' is predicable of God. 'God does not exist. He is being-itself beyond essence and existence' (p. 227). Also Tillich denies that God is pure act. 'The God who is *actus purus* is not the living God' (p. 272). On the next page (which is more than usually obscure) he asserts (without explaining the assertion) that there is potentiality, and even negativity, in God's life. Moreover, on p. 259 he affirms that the Christian doctrine of God must contain a 'pantheistic element'. The very substance of God, he says, is present in the world, although God is not identical with the world of which he is the creative Ground. This is a form of panentheism — a word, strangely, that does not appear in the index.

Tillich also gives contrary accounts of God's relation to the finite 'structures of being' of which he is the Ground and meaning. On p. 264 he states that God *is* this structure. Yet on p. 292 he directly contradicts this statement in words that seem to preclude any kind of pantheism, or even panentheism: 'God is neither in another nor in the same space as the world. He is the creative ground of the spatial structure of the world, but he is not bound to the structure, positively or negatively.'

Finally, Tillich's attitude to the idea of divine personality is ambivalent. Although he stresses that God is the 'living' God, and that 'Spirit' is an all-inclusive symbol of him, he also says that God cannot be called a 'self' (p. 270). On the next page he contents himself with saying that God 'carries within himself the ontological power of personality', and that 'he is not less than personal'.

4. *Object of ultimate concern.* Being-itself (= the Ground of being = God) is also the Object of ultimate concern.

At the beginning of this book Tillich formulates the following theses: '*The object of theology is what concerns us ultimately. Only those propositions are theological which deal with their object in so far as it can become a matter of ultimate concern for us*' (54). '*Our ultimate concern is that which determines our being or non-being. Only those statements are theological which deal with their object in so far as it can become a matter of being or non-being for us*' (55). In

126

viewing God as the Object of human concern theology differs from philosophy, which deals with him purely 'in himself' (pp. 25 and 27). Hence 'revelation is the manifestation of what concerns us ultimately' (p. 123).

Moreover, since everyone has an ultimate concern everyone has a 'god'. 'Whatever concerns a man ultimately becomes god for him' (p. 234). Consequently one can include in theism various non-theistic religions. 'If God is understood as that which concerns man ultimately, early Buddhism has a concept of God just as certainly as has Vedanta Hinduism' (p. 244).

Yet Tillich does not finally wish to say that *anything* can be an Object of ultimate concern. It is only Being-itself that is the true Object of such concern. He states this emphatically with reference to Otto's idea of 'the holy'. 'Only that which is holy can give man ultimate concern' (p. 239). 'The secular is the realm of preliminary concerns. It lacks ultimate concern; it lacks holiness' (p. 241).

Three further points must be noted, although they strictly fall outside my province.

First, Tillich pursues what he calls a 'method of correlation'. By this he means that theology answers the questions that philosophy raises through its reflection on the nature of existence. 'The arguments for the existence of God neither are arguments nor are they proof of the existence of God. They are expressions of the *question* of God which is implied in human finitude' (p. 228). The *answer* can be given only by revelation. And anything can 'enter into a revelatory correlation' (p. 131).

Secondly, Tillich affirms that the human mind is by nature capable of possessing an intuition or experience of unconditioned being through the 'ontological' (in contrast with the 'technical') form of reason. One can call such direct apprehension 'insight' and 'gnosis' (56).

Lastly, Christ is the criterion of every revelation and religious experience. 'The final revelation, the revelation in Jesus as the Christ, is universally valid, because it includes the criterion of every revelation and is the *finis* or *telos* (intrinsic aim) of all of them' (p. 152) (57).

As the previous quotation shows, Tillich writes as a Christian theologian; so that it is on this score that he must be judged. Obviously he retains many essential elements in Christian theism. As I have shown, he often speaks of God as the personal and self-sufficient Ground of the universe. A Christian theist must also endorse his further claim that God, as the ineffably holy one, is the Object of our ultimate concern. The God of the Bible is 'the living God' who constitutes the only answer to the existential questions posed by our finitude. Tillich, in spite of his stylistic defects, expounds these truths with a conviction that explains the influence he has exercised on so many people (58).

Nevertheless, his concept of God is exposed to the following criticisms.

1. Tillich is inconsistent in both affirming that God is Being-itself and denying that 'existence' can be ascribed to him. Certainly God's existence infinitely transcends all finite forms of existence; for he alone is self-existent. He is not 'an' existent entity any more than he is 'a' being. As Gilson affirms in the sentence I quoted in Chapter 1, God is individuated, not by being one among many finite entities, but by being infinite. If we are thinking of finite existence we must say that God is 'beyond existence'. Equally, if we are thinking of finite being we must say that he is 'beyond being'.

The trouble with 'being' (in both its finite and divine significations) is that it can refer to either essence or existence — to either *what* a thing is or *that* it is. It is clear that when Tillich calls God 'Being-itself' he does not intend the first signification. He does not mean the essence of God. He is not abstracting from God's existence either by considering him merely as an 'imaginary focus' of human ideals or by placing his existence in abeyance in the manner advocated by phenomenologists. He means that God *exists*. That this is his meaning is clear, not only by continuous implication, but also by two precise facts: first his assent to the scholastic concept of *aseitas*, and secondly his assertion that 'Being-itself' is the non-symbolical basis of all symbolical descriptions (59).

128

Therefore, in saying that God is 'Being-itself' Tillich is not saying anything that is not included in classical theists' affirmations concerning God's self-existence (or possession of existence and essence in identity). 'Being-itself' is a neologism that does not advance theistic reasoning one iota. It does nothing except introduce a confusion between the two, logically distinct questions: 'What is X?', and 'Does X exist *per se* (and, in the case under consideration, *a se*)'?

2. Tillich inconsistently affirms on the one hand that God is Being-itself (who as such possesses *aseitas*), and on the other hand that there is an element of potentiality in his nature. He does not attempt to overcome this inconsistency by distinguishing (in the manner of Whitehead and Hartshorne) between two natures in God. He does not even seem to see that there is a metaphysical problem there (60).

3. Tillich fails to clarify his views on the personal symbols that theists apply to God. In the end he leaves us in doubt whether God is personal, and, if so, whether he is personal throughout the whole range of his being. According to A. J. McKelway, Tillich holds that 'God transcends the personal, but he nonetheless includes it' (61). This interpretation of Tillich is, I think, correct. But the idea of a God who is both personal and supra-personal is exposed to objections that I stated in my third section on 'Classical theism' (and that I restated with reference to Radhakrishnan).

4. Tillich also fails to clarify the relation of God to the world. At some times he affirms the doctrine of creation; but at other times his language is monistic; and on at least one occasion he explicitly affirms that a true theology must include elements of pantheism. Similarly he says both that God is identical with and that he transcends finite structures of being. He does not seem to be aware of the apparent contradictions which these statements involve.

5. Tillich's use of the expressions 'ultimate concern' and 'Object of ultimate concern' is exposed to the following objections.

(a) Tillich frequently assumes that all men have an Object of ultimate concern — that they all have one supreme and overriding aim or goal. But this is not true. Many people have

129

a number of interests which they only partly harmonise and to none of which they attach supreme importance or worth. They are instances of Plato's 'democratic' man, who pursues now one, now another, goal without any final purpose or integrating vision.

(b) In any case, even if a person does have an Object of ultimate concern, it need not be God (or a metaphysical equivalent to God in a non-theistic system). The object may be a purely secular one (for example, power or wealth). Tillich in fact admits this when he writes that 'whatever concerns a man ultimately becomes god for him'.

However, this is a substitute use of 'God'. It is god (with a small 'g') or 'God' (in inverted commas). When we say of someone who devotes his life to the acquisition of wealth that 'he makes money his god', we mean that he falsely chooses a temporal and finite thing instead of the eternal and infinite God as the final object of his existence. Hence we cannot identify the Object of ultimate concern with God *simpliciter* (62).

Yet Tillich persists in equating 'the object of ultimate concern' with 'God'. Here is a passage from one of his sermons:

> If that word ['God'] has not much meaning for you, translate it, and speak of the depths of your life, of the source of your being, of your ultimate concern, of what you take seriously without any reservation. For if you know that God means depth, you know much about him. You cannot then call yourself an atheist or unbeliever. For you cannot think or say: Life has no depth. Life itself is shallow. Being itself is surface only. If you could say this in complete seriousness, you would be an atheist; but otherwise you are not. He who knows about depth knows about God (63).

In the same sermon Tillich makes the same equation with reference to the socio-political sphere:

> Let us plunge more deeply into the ground of our

130

historical life, into the ultimate depth of history. The name of this infinite and inexhaustible ground of history is *God*. That is what the word means, and it is that to which the words *Kingdom of God* and *Divine Providence* point. And if these words do not have much meaning for you, translate them and speak of the depth of history, of the ground and aim of our social life, and of what you take seriously without reservation in your moral and political activities (64).

In reply to these two quotations it is enough to reiterate the points I have just made. First, it is simply not true that everyone sees a 'deeper' meaning in life under 'the surface', a 'reality' hidden behind the appearances. Many people live continuously in the superficial manner that Tillich rightly condemns. Secondly, even if they do perceive a deeper meaning in events, this meaning need not be a theistic one. Thus (to take the second quotation) many interpretations of history are non-theistic and even (as in the case of Marxism) anti-theistic.

(c) In fact Tillich affirms explicitly, in words I have already quoted, that only 'the holy' is the true Object of ultimate concern. The secular, he says, is the realm of preliminary concerns. The relation between 'the holy' and 'ultimate concern' is asymmetrical. The holy is (or ought to be) the Object of ultimate concern; but not every Object of ultimate concern is holy.

(d) Even if we define 'the Object of ultimate concern' in terms of 'the holy' our definition is still incomplete until we have decided between the following possibilities.

First, 'the holy' need not be God. When Tillich says that early Buddhism and Vedanta Hinduism contain the idea of God because they contain the idea of the Supernatural as the Object of man's ultimate concern he is using the word 'God' irresponsibly. Even if he wishes to apply 'God' to those descriptions of the Supernatural that are, according to common usage, regarded as non-theistic, at least he ought to make it clear that they differ from the descriptions of God offered in the Judaeo-Christian tradition.

131

Secondly, 'ultimate', in a religious context, can be variously interpreted. It can mean that one is concerned with God only in the last resort, when all finite explanations and resources fail. This is the view sometimes held of 'the high god' in primitive religions, and even of the Judaeo-Christian God by casual or uninstructed believers. But Tillich plainly does not mean this; he intends us to see God in and through the secular as the latter's creative Ground and final significance.

(e) Tillich fails to distinguish between the degrees in which God can be spoken of as the Object of our ultimate concern. Like Bultmann he implies that all theological statements must have an immediate and obvious bearing on our existential situation as creatures who are constantly threatened by 'non-being'. But surely we make many theological statements simply in order to satisfy our desire for objective truth or to furnish material for disinterested worship. Indeed, without this desire and without this worship we could not know God as the One who meets our existential needs. But here I encroach on the general nature of religion — a subject beyond my present scope.

This account of Tillich shows that it is impossible to 'label' him. One can quote passages from his writings to support theism, pantheism and panentheism. This syncretism is made metaphysically plausible by a persistent ambiguity in key-terms — especially the term 'Ground of being'. 'Ground' can be taken in so many ways. It can (and in traditional theism often does) signify a personal Creator. It can also signify an Absolute that is conceived pantheistically or panentheistically. Furthermore, such an Absolute may be conceived either as an intelligible Totality or as a supra-rational Unity. Finally 'Ground' (particularly when associated with 'depth') can be used existentially to mean anything that is an Object of ultimate concern. If this object is taken to signify a supernatural Reality it can be interpreted in any one of the preceding ways.

There are difficulties in all concepts of a God who transcends finite phenomena. But the logical difficulties in combining these concepts (as Tillich attempts to do) are insuperable. Moreover, even if the combination were logically possible, it could not be called 'Christian' without a grossly irresponsible piece of linguistic redefinition. To represent it as the quintessence of Protestantism is absurd (65).

Many of the objections I have brought against Tillich can also be brought against J. A. T. Robinson, who, in his widely read 'Honest to God', uses Tillich's terminology to express his intention of revising the traditional Christian concept of God. Since Robinson's book has been rigorously examined by E. L. Mascall in his 'The Secularisation of Christianity' (66), and since I agree with all Mascall's criticisms, I shall briefly assess Robinson's theology in the light of my discussion of theism in general and Tillich's version of it in particular.

Robinson's central thesis is that we must speak of God in terms of 'depth', not 'height'. But he fails to see that the image of depth is insufficient to express Biblical theism unless it is balanced by the image of height. The ambigutiy in his use of 'depth' and the cognate 'Ground' may be seen in the following passages.

Having quoted (on pp. 22 and 47) (67) the two passages from Tillich's sermons that I quoted earlier, Robinson writes on pp. 48-9:

For this way of thinking, to say that 'God is personal' is to say that 'reality at its very deepest level is personal', that personality is of *ultimate* significance in the constitution of the universe. Theological statements are not a description of 'the highest Being' but an analysis of the depths of personal relationships − or, rather, an analysis of the depths of *all* experience 'interpreted by love'.

Now, even if one says − and, of course, many people would deny − that 'love' constitutes the final meaning of life and the Object of ultimate concern, one cannot *identify* human love with divine love without depriving the latter of any distinctive significance. Robinson in fact concedes this point on p. 51 when, having accused John Macmurray of translating theology into anthropology, he observes that such

133

a translation makes the idea of God 'semantically superflous'. On p. 53 he remarks that the author of 1 John wrote 'God is love', not 'love is God'. Still more clearly, he states at the end of the same page that 'the eternal *Thou* is not to be equated with the finite Thou, nor God with man or nature'.

However, on p. 56 Robinson writes thus: 'This, I believe, is Tillich's great contribution to theology — the reinterpretation of transcendence in a way which preserves its reality while detaching it from the projection of supranaturalism. The Divine, as he sees it, does not inhabit a transcendent world *above nature*; it is found in the 'ecstatic' character of *this* world, as its transcendent Depth and Ground.' The idea of God as a transcendent Person who creates and governs the world while remaining himself outside it is a 'myth' that is theologically obsolete (although it may still have a place in liturgy and prayer, for example in the Paternoster) (68).

All theists must agree with Robinson in his protests against an anthropomorphic or a deistic view of God's transcendence. But unless we are prepared to equate God with man or opt for some form of pantheism — and Robinson is not prepared to take either of these courses — we must balance the image of 'depth' by the image of 'height', the idea of immanence by the idea of transcendence. Here we can learn from the mystics. They (in so far as they are distinctively Christian) affirm (as a matter of experience as well as dogma) that the God who dwells in the 'Ground' of the soul is also the unutterably transcendent Lord.

Yet it is God's transcendence that needs stressing in a Tillichian context. No image can be predicated of God literally. All theistic images ('depth' no less than 'height') must be taken symbolically. With this proviso R. W. Hepburn is clearly right in asserting that 'the language of 'transcendence', the thought of God as a personal being wholly other to man is an indispensable element in Christianity' (69).

Robinson fails to clarify these crucial points in his later book — 'Exploration into God' (70). He repudiates an impersonalistic and pantheistic interpretation of the phrase 'Ground of being' (p. 23); but he agrees with Tillich in

134

holding that we should cease to speak of God's 'existence' (p. 39). On the one hand he endorses the Hindu view that we can speak of God only through the *via negativa*; but on the other hand he affirms that we know God as a personal reality in Christ (71). On pp. 67 and 132 he says that we know nothing of God in himself, but that we know him only in his impact on ourselves (72). The nearest he comes to a definitive statement is on pp. 83 and 145, where he opts for 'panentheism'; but he does not amplify the latter term; and on p. 144 he contradicts himself by denying that God includes finite selves.

(f) Macquarrie

I have chosen John Macquarrie's 'Principles of Christian Theology' (73) for two reasons. First, it is the only large-scale work of dogmatic theology to have been written by a British theologian in recent years. Secondly, it represents an attempt to restate Christian theism in terminology derived from existentialism in general and the philosophy of Heidegger in particular (74).

After a penetrating analysis of human existence Macquarrie concludes that the latter raises questions that can be answered only by the revelation of God as 'Being' or 'holy Being' (p. 95). He then proceeds to analyse the idea of Being. After this analysis he returns to, and amplifies, his definition of God.

Macquarrie begins by stating what Being is *not* (75). Being is not itself 'a' being; it is not a property; it is not a class; it is not a substance (that is, 'a substratum supposed to underlie the phenomenal characteristics of being'); it is not 'what philosophers have sometimes called 'the absolute', whether this is conceived as the all-inclusive being or as the totality of beings or as the sum of beings'.

What then *is* Being? The first thing Macquarrie says is that Being must include becoming. 'We can talk about being and distinguish it from nothing only in so far as it includes becoming' (p. 101). Macquarrie intends this dictum to apply

135

to God as much as to any finite being. Hence on p. 190 he asserts that God is not immutable or changeless; for 'without becoming we could not know about any being, nor could there be anything like holy Being'.

Macquarrie then interprets the concept of Being through concept of 'Letting-be'. 'Being, strictly speaking, 'is' not; but being 'lets be', and since letting-be is prior to particular instances of being, though other than these, we are justified in claiming that being is more beingful than any particular being that it lets be, and we have justification too for using, with proper care and qualification, the expression 'being is' ' (p. 103). Macquarrie adds that 'letting-be' does not mean (according to ordinary usage) 'leaving alone'. On the contrary, it means 'something much more positive and active, as enabling to be, empowering to be, or bringing into being'.

'Letting-be' can be further understood through the notions of 'presence' and 'manifestation'. We know Being through its presence or manifestation in particular beings. Being is more fully present or manifest in the higher than in the lower beings on the evolutionary scale. 'An atom of hydrogen, for instance, and a well-integrated human self are both beings that manifest being; but the self manifests being much more fully than the atom' (p. 104).

God, as 'holy Being', is the ultimate power that 'lets be'; for he creates and sustains all things by his *fiat*. Hence he merits our worship and obedience. Macquarrie believes that he and Otto agree in their phenomenological analysis. 'Our final analysis of being as the *incomparable* that *lets-be* and is *present-and-manifest*, is strikingly parallel to the analysis of the numinous as *mysterium tremendum et fascinans*' (p. 105).

Macquarrie sees his terminology as the last stage in a process of theistic purification. 'At the *mythological* level, God was conceived anthropomorphically as a being much like ourselves, only more powerful, and he 'dwelt' in a definite place, the top of a mountain, perhaps, or the sky' (p. 106). Although traditional theism toned down or symbolically explained anthropomorphic elements, it still regarded God as 'another being in addition to the beings we know in the

136

world' (ibid.). Macquarrie claims that his 'existential-ontological theism', in finally eliminating the idea of God as 'a' being who exists alongside other beings, imparts to this idea a uniqueness and ultimacy that it did not previously possess.

Macquarrie is very anxious to leave a place for genuine atheism. 'Atheism is the denial of the holiness of being, and consequently the denial that man should have faith in being or take up the attitude of acceptance and commitment before being' (p. 108). Also (as we have seen already) (76) Macquarrie firmly repudiates pantheism. 'Being not only is not *a* being, but it is not the sum of beings or the totality of beings or an all-inclusive being. Being 'is' the *transcendens*, and this term indicates not only God's distinction from the world but his 'wholly other' character as over against whatever is within the world' (p. 109).

What properties, then, does God possess? Macquarrie has already ascribed holiness to God, and in the course of this book he adds most of the other properties that are attributed to God in Christianity. On p. 126 he justifies the attribution through the concept of analogy:

> Surely the understanding of Being that has been set out in earlier sections of this theology enables us to interpret the *analogia entis* in a way that will neither assimilate God to man nor yet put an unbridgeable gulf between them. Being has been called an incomparable and a *transcendens*, and there could be no beings without the Being that lets them be; but Being is present and manifest in the beings; and apart from the beings Being would become indistinguishable from nothing. Hence Being and the beings, though neither can be assimilated to the other, cannot be separated from each other either. This ontological doctrine corresponds to the religious experience of the holy as at once *tremendum* and *fascinosum*, as characterised by otherness and closeness.

Macquarrie then offers two criteria for choosing between theistic symbols. We must choose those which have been

137

specially revealed and those which express the greatest degree of Being. Both these criteria entail the primacy of symbols drawn from the sphere of human existence. The first criterion entails it because God's revelation in Christ (which is the 'primordial' one for Christians) is personal in all its aspects. The second criterion entails it because persons 'are entities having the widest range of participation in Being and so best able to symbolise it' (p. 131).

In many ways Macquarrie is faithful to the Christian tradition that he seeks to reinterpret. Aquinas would certainly have agreed that God is, not 'a' being, but Being *simpliciter*. He would also have agreed that the analogy of being permits analogical descriptions of God's nature. Macquarrie further shows his affinity with theism in his rejection of pantheism, and his assignment of primacy to personal symbols in theistic discourse. He also has many valuable things to say on matters that fall outside my appointed scope (77).

However, I am obliged to raise the following queries and objections.

1. Macquarrie fails to distinguish sufficiently between Being in the sense of essence and Being in the sense of existence — between *what* a thing is and *that* it is. Maritain formulates this distinction thus:

> *Being* in the sense of *existence* and being in the sense of *essence* belong to two distinct categories. The term being has two wholly different meanings. For example, in the quotation 'to be or not to be, that is the question', being means *existence*, but on the contrary in the phrase *a living being* it means *essence*. In the first case the term *being* signifies the *act* of being, the act, if I may so put it, which posits a thing outside nonentity, and outside its causes (*extra nihil, extra causas*); and in the second case it signifies *that* which is or may be, that which corresponds to some existence, actual or possible (78).

2. Macquarrie fails to distinguish sharply enough between the idea or concept of X and X's existence. I can have a

138

concept of X's essence or nature although it does not exist. I can even conceive of it as existing (and explicitly judge that it exists) although it does not exist. In the case of God I can even conceive of it as *necessarily* existing (and explicitly judge that it exists) although there is no logical contradiction in denying that it thus exists. The absence of this contradiction invalidates the ontological argument in all its forms.

3. I do not, of course, wish to imply that Macquarrie is unfamiliar with these distinctions or that he would dissent from them. But I suggest that his failure to make them and to give them prominence is responsible for the prevarication and obscurity of his remarks on the question of God's existence. I could conceive God's nature (within the limits imposed by analogy) even if he did not exist. Moreover (as I have just observed), I could conceive him as *necessarily* existing even if he did not exist. The most that the idea of a necessary being entails is that *if* God exists he exists necessarily; but no argument can dispel the 'if'.

The crucial passage is on p. 108. Having pointed out (rightly) that God does not exist as a finite being exists, Macquarrie concludes thus: 'It can be asserted that, while to say 'God exists' is strictly inaccurate and may be misleading if it makes us think of him as *some* being or other, yet it is more appropriate to say 'God exists' than 'God does not exist', since God's letting-be is prior to and the condition of the existence of any particular being.' I fail to understand Macquarrie's hesitation. If we refuse to state outright 'God exists', we must state 'God has independent reality'; but the second statement is equivalent to the first. The simple question (which A. E. Taylor took as the title of his last book) 'Does God exist?' is as relevant as ever.

4. Macquarrie's use of 'being' as a term through which to signify both God and finite entities obscures the truth of God's transcendence. Admittedly Macquarrie sometimes indicates the transcendence of God's being by the use of a capital 'B' and by the adjective 'holy'. Yet a stronger indication is necessary in order to avoid giving the impression of pantheism or panentheism. Even Tillich's 'Being-itself' is

139

an improvement. But if one is to be absolutely clear one ought to preface being (and even Being) by 'self-existent' or 'infinite'. The importance of this point will be seen in my next criticism (79).

5. In his use of the concept 'Letting-be' Macquarrie makes an unwarranted transition from finite to infinite being. On p. 103 (in the course of discussing the idea of being in general), having said that being transcends all categories, he asks how it should be described. After considering 'energy' and 'act' he decides that it is best described through the concept of 'Letting-be'. He explains this concept thus: 'In ordinary English usage, to 'let be' often means to leave alone, to refrain from interfering. This is not the sense that is intended here. By 'Letting-be' I mean something much more positive and active, as enabling to be, empowering to be, or bringing into being.'

However, this sense of 'Letting-be' applies only to God as the Creator; and it is obvious that this is the application Macquarrie intends. Hence on p. 105 he says that his analysis of being leads to the idea of God as *the incomparable* that *lets-be* and is *present-and-manifest*'. Again, after explaining his reluctance to ascribe 'existence' to God, he asserts that 'God (or being) *is* not, but rather *lets be*' (p. 108).

Two things need to be said here. First, it is misleading to define being in general in terms of 'Letting-be'. Only God (*qua* infinite being) 'lets be'; all finite beings are the results of his (creative) 'Letting-be'. Secondly, a neutral analysis of finite beings does not lead by logical necessity to the idea of an infinite being who is present in them and who 'lets them be'. An atheist could validly reply that so far as he can see finite beings simply are (existentially) as they are (essentially), and that there is no logical compulsion to posit a 'holy' Being that 'lets them be' by his immanent and creative power.

Macquarrie's application of 'Letting-be' to being in general is both ontologically and logically illicit. It is ontologically so because only one being (God) can 'let be'. It is logically so because it implies that a neutral analysis of finite beings must lead to the idea of their divine ground.

140

6. Macquarrie holds that change and becoming must be predicated of God. On p. 191 he goes so far as to say that Being 'expands and realises itself in history'. But he does not examine the reasons that have led classical theists to affirm that God is pure Act. Also he does not make it clear whether God changes in all respects (80). Finally, his only ground for postulating change in God is questionable. On p. 101 he asserts that because becoming implies Being (for 'whatever becomes must, in some sense, *already be*') Being implies becoming; but the assertion is not self-evident; and we are not offered any demonstration of its truth.

Conclusion

The preceding chapters have shown that concepts of God differ in the following five main ways.

1. *Infinity or finiteness.* Classical theists affirm that God is infinite. By this they mean, not that he is formless or characterless (or that he is a 'magnified man'), but that his being is free from all creaturely limitations. God's infinity means, basically, his self-existence. Whereas the existence of each finite entity is conditioned by factors external to itself, his existence is unconditioned or absolute. Plato's Demiurge, on the other hand, is limited both by the Forms and by matter. Similarly Aristotle's God is, though the final, not the efficient, cause of the world. Within this century Whitehead held that God and the world create each other: God creates the world by being its principle of limitation, and the world creates God by contributing to his consequent nature.

2. *Being and becoming.* Classical theists affirm that God is pure Being. Pantheists, however, are bound to predicate becoming of God in so far as they hold that he expresses himself in this world of change. The most striking example is Hegel, who interpreted history as the self-development of the Absolute. The postulation of growth in one aspect or pole of God's nature is a distinctive element in the so-called 'process theology' of Whitehead and Hartshorne. Macquarrie also maintains that God is characterised by becoming as well as being.

3. *Existence.* The ascription of existence (in the unique form of self-existence) to God is the basis of classical theism. But some thinkers (notably Tillich and Macquarrie) are reluctant to assert 'God exists', lest the assertion suggests that God is one (albeit the highest) among many beings. Hence
142

they prefer to speak of him as Being. Similarly Radhakrishnan affirms that God is a universal reality who is beyond existence and non-existence.

4. *Personality.* Is God personal? There are three possible answers to this question. On the one hand some affirm (with Barth and Brunner) that God is *per se* and throughout his being personal. Although classical theists do not always explicity state that God is thus personal they state it implicitly by asserting that he essentially possesses spiritual properties that can be attributed to him by an 'analogy of proportionality'. On the other hand others affirm (with Sankara and F. H. Bradley) that the Absolute entirely transcends personal categories. Others, again, seek a mediating position by holding that God is not less than personal or that he is personal in relation to us.

5. *God's relation to the world.* According to classical theism God creates the world *ex nihilo*. According to those who regard him as finite he acts as a final and formal cause in relation to a material substrate that exists independently of him. According to Plotinus the world emanates from him in decreasingly real degrees without diminishing his plentitude. Classical theists hold that God does not need the world that he creates through an overflowing of the perfect love that he enjoys within his triune life. But pantheists and panentheists are obliged to hold that the world is as necessary to God as God is to the world. Panentheists differ from pantheists (in the strict sense of the word) in holding that an element in God transcends and is independent of the world. Some panentheists (for example Pringle-Pattison) leave this element unspecified; but others (especially Whitehead and Hartshorne) attempt to define it.

In particular the following divine attributes have been variously interpreted.

(a) *Eternity.* In classical theism God's eternity is interpreted as timelessness, which (it is held) is entailed by his self-existence. But the idea of a timeless being has been attacked on various grounds (for example, on the ground that

143

it is incompatible with the idea of personality). Consequently some theologians are content with the assertion that in an unspecifiable way God transcends, and so is sovereign over, temporal processes.

(b) *Omniscience*. It is widely agreed that God knows all things that can be known. But does he know them in a timeless present or does he know them as succesive? Also, does he foreknow or know in a *totum simul* all the free choices that his creatures make? Even orthodox Christian theists differ in the answers they give to these questions.

(c) *Immutability*. Ever since St Augustine it has been an axiom of Christian theism that God cannot change. Yet if he imparts a share of his substance to the world he is bound to change *pro tanto* with it. That God changes in one aspect of his nature in response to the world is a central tenet in the non-monistic panentheism advocated by Whitehead and Hartshorne.

(d) *Impassibility*. In its general sense this is equivalent to immutability. But in its particular sense it means that God cannot experience pain. According to the main tradition of Christian theism God is impassible in the second as well as the first sense. But many theists, as well as panentheists, hold that the absence of suffering in God would be incompatible with his perfect love.

At the present time controversy is focused on the following three points.

First, there is the question whether God is immutable or characterised by change and becoming. Here it is necessary to bear the following points in mind.

(i) The problem of being and becoming has been a primary metaphysical one ever since the Greeks, and various solutions of it are still given. Moreover, a discussion of it in relation to God cannot be separated from a discussion of it in relation to finite entities; for the ascription of either being or becoming to God can be justified only by comparison and contrast with, or by a limiting concept derived from, creatures.

(ii) One cannot credibly assert that God is *merely* becoming, *merely* process. It is obvious even on the

144

finite plane that the Heraclitan maxim πάντα ρεî is untenable. All change and becoming imply some form of changeless being in the object of which change is predicated. Hence Hartshorne is obliged to postulate an 'aspect' of God that is changeless.

(iii) We need not identify the changelessness that classical theists attribute to God with an impersonal or static state of being. From the beginning Christian theists have identified God's actuality with the Biblical revelation of his personal energy. Here, as elsewhere, both Augustinian and Thomist philosophical theology has been, in intention, an activity of *fides quaerens intellectum*.

(iv) To repeat a point I made earlier, we must distinguish between 'change' and response'. To say that X changes is to say that it is definably different at t2 from what it was at t1. To say that a spiritual being changes is to say that it is spiritually better or worse at t2 than at t1 − that it is more or less good, more or less powerful, more or less wise. Theists assert that in this sense God (*qua* self-existent being) *cannot* change. At the same time they assert that God, out of his changeless wisdom, love and power, perfectly *responds to* his creatures in all their circumstances and needs. Moreover, they assert that he can perfectly respond *because* he is changeless.

Secondly, there is the question of divine impassibility. The traditional view of classical theism is that God cannot experience pain; for if he did so he would be capable of change in response to his creatures and would lack the absolute joy that is a mark of his perfection. Hence Christian theists have affirmed that Christ suffered in his human, but not his divine, nature. Yet the objections to this view are grave. If God is perfect love, how can he be untouched by our sins and sufferings? If he became fully Man, how could he not have been acquainted with the sufferings he endured in his manhood as the price of our salvation? I have suggested that it is possible to combine the view that God really shares our sufferings with the view that in sharing them he remains

145

changeless. At the same time I wish to stress two complementary points. On the one hand Christians who affirm God's impassibility also affirm his love — his infinitely active concern and pity for all his creatures. The only question is whether the two affirmations are compatible. On the other hand, if we wish to combine belief in God's capacity to experience pain with belief in his immutability, we must admit that we can provide only a faint human symbol of the combination.

Thirdly, there is the question of God's personality. Just as the question of God's immutability has been raised with new force by Whitehead and Hartshorne, so the question of his personality has been raised by various thinkers in both the East and West (notably Radhakrishnan and Tillich). Here it is particularly obvious that if our theology is to be acceptable it must satisfy both metaphysical and religious requirements.

Two further points of a general kind must be borne in mind.

First, in considering these various concepts of God we must be cautious in applying classificatory terms. As we have seen, even would-be pantheists write sometimes, implicitly or explicitly, in a panentheistic vein. Again, those who are theists in the basic sense that they repudiate pantheism and panentheism disagree in crucial matters. Thus Barth's dipolar statements concerning God distinguish him from Aquinas and place him with Hartshorne although there are no traces of panentheism in his theology. How too are we to classify the doctrine of a finite God? We cannot do so *a priori*; for it can take both a theistic form (as in the case of Mill) and a panentheistic form (as in the case of Whitehead). Finally, even theists who reject dipolarism and affirm that God is the Creator of all things differ in the degrees to which they approximate to the classical theism of Aquinas (1).

Secondly, many non-theists have claimed that their systems are consonant with Christianity. Thus Pringle-Pattison maintained that his Hegelianism expressed the true meaning of the Trinity, the Incarnation and the Atonement. Similarly Tillich held that his philosophically syncretistic description of God in terms of Being represented the essence

146

of Christian truth. Most recently J. A. T. Robinson has affirmed that the Christian concept of God can be given a panentheistic interpretation. From a Hindu standpoint Radhakrishnan has claimed that the true meaning of Christ emerges when he is seen, monistically, as one among the higher manifestations of the one ineffable Brahman (2).

In concluding I shall raise three questions. I can do no more than indicate, on the basis of the preceding chapters, the answers I should give to them.

1. Are there grounds for preferring one concept to other concepts of God? I believe that there are the following grounds for preferring classical theism.

(a) Pantheists and panentheists fall into self-contradiction by attributing mutually exclusive properties to God. In the case of pantheism Stace admits the contradiction. The two most influential panentheists of this century differ. Although Whitehead admits that dipolarism is paradoxical he affirms, without explanation, that it is not self-contradictory. Hartshorne offers two explanations. But these do not succeed; they lead to further contradictions; and in any case they are incompatible with each other.

Admittedly, classical theists have sometimes been accused of making self-contradictory statements. In my view this accusation always rests on either a false assumption or a failure to make a necessary distinction. Thus those who claim that the idea of necessary being is self-contradictory can do so only by assuming either that 'necessity' applies always to concepts and never to things, or that if God's being is ontologically necessary the affirmation of his existence must be logically so. Both these assumptions are arbitrary. Again, critics of theism sometimes fail to distinguish between different senses of 'incomprehensibility'. X may be incomprehensible either because it involves a logically inconsistent use of concepts, or because, though it does not involve such a use, it transcends our powers of understanding. I have maintained that whereas the paradoxes of pantheism and panentheism are incomprehensible in the first sense, the paradoxes of theism are so in the second.

Certainly it is not always easy to distinguish between an

apparent and a real contradiction. Certainly, too, the application of opposing predicates to the same entity need not involve a self-contradiction. Thus we can describe a human person through the diverse categories of unity and multiplicity, being and becoming, permanence and change. We can do so because we are applying these categories in finite, relative modes to finite individuals. But panentheists' application of infinity and finiteness to the same entity is a manifest self-contradiction; for the first member of this pair by its nature excludes the other. It is Stace's great merit that he frankly admits the contradiction and rejects Hegel's attempt to 'resolve' it in a 'higher' logic.

(b) Although the God of theism transcends our understanding there are analogies to him in our finite form of being. Thus, although we cannot understand how God, being self-sufficient, creates the world, we can rationally postulate his creative act as the supreme instance of a disinterested, overflowing generosity that even we are capable of partially expressing. Furthermore, let us take the most difficult case — the claim which I have made that God simultaneously experiences and transforms his creatures' sufferings. Even this claim has a basis in our knowledge of the manner in which saintly characters maintain their serenity and peace amid those very evils to which they are more sensitive than most of us can ever be (3).

Yet panentheists fail to provide analogies for their two distinctive tenets. First, there cannot in the nature of things be any finite analogy to the union of infinity and finiteness in the same entity. This would have to be admitted even by those who do not find dipolarism logically incoherent. We can point to the whole range of human spirituality and say: 'Free this of its limitations and you have the infinite being of God.' But we cannot say of anything: 'Free this of its limitations and you have a combination of the limited and the unlimited.' Also panentheists cannot adduce any human analogy for their claim that the divine self includes human selves; for (as Pringle-Pattison incongruously admitted) the very nature of a human self is to be impermeable by other selves. Whereas theists posit in God an infinite exempli-

148

fication of properties that human selves possess in varying degrees, panentheists posit in him an all-inclusiveness that is at variance with the essence of selfhood.

I wish to stress strongly that all concepts of God are open to query; that all, at some point or points, permit different interpretations; and that all involve, in the end, an element of mystery. Yet I maintain that, purely from the standpoint of conceptual analysis, theism is preferable to pantheism and panentheism on three grounds. First, unlike pantheism and panentheism, theism does not involve the application of inherently opposing predicates to God. To say that God is infinitely wise and loving is to affirm one kind of mystery; to say that he is both infinite and finite is to affirm another. The first is an affirmation of what is inconceivable because we lack the mental powers to conceive it; the second is the affirmation of what is inconceivable *per se*. Secondly, whereas theists can, pantheists and panentheists cannot, provide pointers to (or in I. T. Ramsey's terminology, qualified models of) their distinctive affirmations concerning the divine *mysterium*. Thirdly, and as a consequence, when there is doubt concerning the mutual consistency of theistic statements the doubt is, logically, different in kind from the perplexity aroused by the paradoxes of dipolarism. To doubt whether God can experience pain is to doubt whether *in this one respect* finite love has an infinite analogate. To be perplexed by Hartshorne's assertion that God is both infinite and finite is to be perplexed by an ascription to the same subject of predicates that *by their very definition and throughout the whole range of their possible applications* exclude each other.

(c) Only theism answers all the questions raised by natural theology. Even if Whitehead's God can account for the order and apparent design in nature it cannot explain the bare existence of finite things. Yet, as Wittgenstein observed in the often-quoted words at the end of his 'Tractatus', the final mystery of the world is constituted not by *what* it is but by *that* it is. The only final explanation of anything is that it is created and sustained by self-existent Being. Furthermore, the idea of a pre-existent matter on which God operates is very enigmatic. I should also maintain that only theism can answer the ultimate questions raised by morality (4).

(d) Only theism can accomodate all those modes of experience that, on purely phenomenological grounds, can be called distinctively religious. Thus, although both theism and monism can take forms that are commonly called 'mystical', only theism can justify the feeling of absolute dependence and the sense of the numinous. Likewise, although Whitehead's theology enables us to look on God as our Friend, it does not justify us in offering him unconditioned adoration, or permit us to hope in him as the source of our personal immorality. Again, although Plotinus and Spinoza exhort us to love God, they forbid us to regard him as a personal being who answers our prayers and grants us his grace.

(e) *Christian* theists claim that their view of God, together with the paradoxes it entails, is a response to his special revelation recorded in the Scriptures. The basic *revelata* are God's unity, personality, transcendence, creativity and moral holiness. Belief in these divine attributes is professed by Jews and Christians alike. Christians further believe that through Christ as the incarnate Word God reveals himself as a triunity — as Father, Son and Holy Spirit (5). But pantheists and panentheists do not claim any revealed basis for their distinctive tenets, which are based on purely speculative reasoning.

2. The second question is the one that has chiefly occupied philosophers of religion in recent years. If God is, as theists assert, infinite, can we, as finite beings, make meaningful statements concerning him? I have suggested that we can do so by recourse to the doctrine of analogy. If we posit an 'analogy of being' between the Creator and the creature we can speak of the Creator in creaturely terms through an 'analogy of proportionality'. But I must leave a further discussion of religious language to other writers in this series.

3. Are there grounds for believing that God exists? Even if the theistic concept of him is rationally superior to any other, do we have good reasons for believing that the concept has an instance? Although I have referred to the possible

150

grounds of belief I have not been able to assess their validity. I must leave this question also to my fellow-authors (6).

Notes

INTRODUCTION

1. 'Five Stages of Greek Religion' (Watts, 1943) p. 12.

CHAPTER 1

1. *Diaspora* means 'dispersion' and refers to Jews living outside Palestine.

2. A group of Christian theologians who wrote c. 120-220.

3. The (first) Council of Nicaea was in 325.

4. I shall quote both from the new Blackfriars edition (which I shall use unless I indicate otherwise) and from the two anthologies entitled 'Philosophical Texts' and 'Theological Texts', ed. T. Gilby (Oxford University Press, 1951 and 1955).

5. The name given to the author of Isaiah 40-55.

6. 1 Cor. 8:5-6.

7. 'ST' la 11, 3.

8. For such a discussion, see the volume in this series on 'Arguments for the Existence of God'.

9. The Christian Trinity and the Plotinian Triad also differ in their structure. The members of the former are, but the members of the latter are not, coequal. I shall discuss Plotinus later.

10. 'God and Philosophy' (Hutchinson, 1966) p. 47.

11. 'ST' la 7, 1.

12. 'New Essays in Philosophical Theology', ed. A. Flew and A. Macintyre (S.C.M. Press, 1963) p. 68. Hick has shown that the failure to distinguish between ontological and logical necessity vitiates Malcolm's reformulation of the ontological argument ('The Many-Faced Argument' Macmillan, 1968 pp. 341-56).

13. In his 'De Consolatione', 5.

14. 'ST' 1a 10, 1.

15. 'Timaeus', 37 D.

16. Mal. 3:6 (quoted by Aquinas in 'ST' 1a 9, 1).

17. So far as revelation is concerned, we have a symbol of this divine transfiguration in the manner in which the Johannine Christ (as the incarnate Word) associates 'glory' with his Passion.

18. 'ST' 1a 3, 7, trans. Gilby, 'Philosophical Texts', 188.

19. 1 'Contra Gentiles', 31, trans. Gilby, ibid., 189.

20. 'ST' 1a 4, 3.

21. 1 'Contra Gentiles', 57, trans. Gilby, 'Philosophical Texts', 297.

22. The problems I have stated become even more acute when they are raised with reference to the Incarnation.

23. 'Opusc.' 26, 'de Rationibus Fidei', trans. Gilby, 'Philosophical Texts', 310.

24. For another statement of the view that God, though in himself timeless, knows the world as a temporal succession, see G. F. Stout's 'God and Nature' (Cambridge University Press, 1952) pp. 222-30.

25. I cannot here discuss the scholastic doctrine (inherited from Neo-Platonism via Augustine) that evil is 'a privation of good'. It is enough to observe that those who adhere to the doctrine affirm the full reality of evil, and that we still have to explain how the privation arose.

26. (Macmillan, 1966). There are two further problems connected with the idea of divine omnipotence that I must also leave to my fellow-writers in this series. First, does belief in God's omnipotence entail universalism (the view that all men will be saved)? Secondly, is theism discredited because (as Flew asserts) it is not falsifiable by the fact of evil? I believe that we must remain agnostic concerning the answer to the first question, and that there is no reason for (but that there are many reasons against) the view that theistic statements must be empirically testable.

27. Is. 55:8.

28. 'ST' 1a 12, 1, trans. Gilby, 'Philosophical Texts', 254.

153

29. 'De Divinis Nominibus', 1, trans. Gilby, 'Theological Texts', 482.

30. Two valuable subsequent studies in the theistic use of 'mystery' are contained in E. L. Mascall's 'Words and Images' (Darton, Longman & Todd, 1968), and H. D. Lewis's essay in 'Prospect for Metaphysics', ed. I. T. Ramsey (Allen & Unwin, 1961).

31. 'Twentieth-Century Religious Thought' (S.C.M. Press, 1963) p. 324.

32. 'ST' la 8, 1, trans. Gilby, 'Philosophical Texts', 234.

33. 'The Elements of Christian Philosophy', Mentor-Omega Books, New American Library, 1960 p. 148.

34. I do not say that all these errors are committed by all theologians who can be called 'existentialist'; but they are all committed by Bultmann, who is the most influential of living existentialists; and they unfortunately obscure his many valuable insights.

35. On the inadequacy of Jaspers and Bultmann in this respect, see Eugene Long's 'Jaspers and Bultmann' (1968).

36. I ought, perhaps, to comment on one further, purely logical, question raised by this analysis. Is 'God' a name or a description? Some philosophers (e.g. Geach in 'Three Philosophers' (Blackwell, 1961) pp. 109-10) hold that it is a description. Others (e.g. Ziff in 'Religious Experience and Truth' ed. Hood (Oliver & Boyd, 1961) pp. 195-202) hold that it is a name. The truth surely is (as Norris Clarke observes in his answer to Ziff, ibid., pp. 224-6) that 'God' has both functions. It is a name in so far as it is used (like 'John' or 'Mary') to denote an individual who can be addressed in prayer and worship. It is a description in so far as we can give its meaning by listing God's properties. Yet it differs from all finite names in so far as the being it denotes is not an individuated essence or member of a class. Equally it differs from all finite descriptions in so far as the properties it connotes can have only one referent. The ways in which 'God' names and describes are logically odd; but they are logically acceptable if the concept of God as a unique being is metaphysically valid.

CHAPTER 2

1. I shall discuss Whitehead's thought in detail in my section on 'Process theology'.

2. 'Religion in the Making' (Cambridge University Press, 1926) pp. 154-5.

3. 'Process and Reality' (Cambridge University Press, 1929) p. 490.

4. 'A Christian Natural Theology' (Lutterworth Press, 1966) p. 211.

5. 'Science and the Modern World' (Cambridge University Press, 1926) pp. 221-2. The ontological status of Whitehead's 'eternal objects' is also very enigmatic.

6. It is even more obvious that the doctrine of a finite god has no room for mysticism of either a theistic or monistic kind; for mysticism in all its forms implies that the object of union is an unconditioned Ground of all that exists.

7. 1 Cor. 8:6; Col. 1:16; Heb. 11:3; and John 1:3.

8. The Neo-Platonists developed various metaphysical and religious elements in Plato's philosophy. Plotinus's thought is contained in 'The Enneads', which I shall quote from Stephen MacKenna's translation (Faber, 1956).

9. Plotinus exercised a great influence on St Augustine and Dionysius the Pseudo-Areopagite, and through them on medieval mystics and theologians.

10. 'Enneads', 5.4.1; 5.5.4; 6.8.11.

11. Ibid., 4.8.6.

12. Ibid., 5.1.7.

13. Ibid., 5.2.1.

14. Ibid., 2.9.4.

15. Ibid., 1.8.8-9; 2.4.6.

16. Ibid., 6.8.13.

17. Ibid., 6.8.9.

18. 'A History of Philosophy', I (Burns & Oates, 1946) 467.

19. *A fortiori* it is meaningless to regard *me-ontic* matter as the source of evil.

20. In his introduction to MacKenna's translation, p. xix.

21. The writings attributed to him were probably

composed at the end of the fifth century.

22. See (for example) the invaluable Blackfriars symposium entitled 'Mystery and Mysticism', and especially A. Léonard's essay (1956).

23. On the Christo-centric nature of Christian mysticism, see ch. 9 of David Knowles's excellent 'What is Mysticism?' (Burns & Oates, 1966).

24. It must be noted that pantheism has been (and still is) widely held in many non-philosophical forms. 'Nature-religion' — belief in a cosmos that is itself divine (or the extension of a divine Reality) — has been present in all cultures.

25. 'Ethics', 1, def. 6. All my references are to this work in Andrew Boyle's translation (Everyman ed., 1959).

26. Ibid., 1, prop. 14.

27. Ibid., 1, prop. 33.

28. Ibid., 2, prop. 11.

29. Ibid., 5, prop. 36.

30. Sankara's teaching, and Hindu monism as a whole, is well summarised by R. C. Zaehner in his 'Hinduism' (Oxford University Press, 1962) ch 2-4. The Western philosopher closest to Sankara is F. H. Bradley, who regarded the world as a mere 'appearance' of the Absolute. It is important to realise that (as Zaehner shows) the monistic element in Hinduism has always coexisted with theistic elements. I shall recur to this point later in this book.

31. Thus Spinoza, although he formally identifies God with the world, implies that the former transcends the latter when he affirms that God loves himself through finite selves and that all things are determined by God's nature; for A cannot love himself through B or C unless his selfhood is distinct from A's and B's, and X cannot determine Y unless it is distinct from Y. At least there must be *some* distinction, *some* form and degree of transcendence of lover over loved and cause over effect. A similar ambiguity in Hegel's thought is noted by Frederick Copleston ('A History of Philosophy', vii, Burns & Oates, 1963) 195-8. Although Hegel speaks as if the Absolute were identical with the Totality, he also implies that it has an element of transcendence. As Copleston

puts it, 'we cannot escape making a distinction between inner and outer, between the one infinite Life, self-actualising Spirit, and the finite manifestations in and through which it lives and has its being' (ibid., p. 198).

32. 'Spinoza' (Penguin Books, 1951) p. 46.

33. 'Philosophy of Religion' (English Universities Press, 1965) p. 209.

34. Cambridge University Press, 1926.

35. Cambridge University Press, 1929.

36. 'Religion in the Making', p. 70.

37. Ibid., pp. 70-1.

38. Ibid., p. 75.

39. Ibid., p. 153. To these five grounds one must add the ground which Whitehead stresses in his 'Science and the Modern World', and which I examined earlier — namely that a God who is both omnipotent and good cannot be the Creator of a world containing evil.

40. Ibid., p. 102, 119-20, 154.

41. In 'Process and Reality' Whitehead also affirms (as we shall see) that God is the world's final cause.

42. The strongest of his objections is the first — that an infinite God is not rationally comprehensible; but he does not mention the attempts that theists have made to solve this problem; and he does not examine any of the difficulties that his own concept of God creates. In answer to his second objection I should maintain that *no* concept of God can be *proved* to have an instance. With reference to the third objection it must of course be admitted that believers in an omnipotent Creator have often conceived him in terms of power, not love. But the authentic Christian claim is that God's power, both within his own uncreated life and in his relation to the world, is identical with his love. The fourth objection — that to be actual is to be limited — is an arbitrary assumption. The fifth — that if God were infinite he would be evil as well as good — is refuted by the fact that evil, in personal beings, is intrinsically limiting; it is a privation of the moral goodness which constitutes their perfection and so (in the teleological sense) their good.

43. Whitehead here draws a parallel with Aristotle's

'unmoved mover'.

44. His own adjective.

45. 'Philosophers Speak of God' (University of Chicago Press, 1953) pp. 282-3. This is an anthology (with comments) of writers representing different concepts of God. Among modern panentheists Hartshorne includes Schelling, Berdyaev, Radhakrishan and Schweitzer. But there is considerable variety in the extent to which these thinkers resemble Hartshorne. Thus Hartshorne is forced to admit that panentheism is only implicit in Schweitzer's thought. The philosopher with whom Hartshorne has the closest affinity is undoubtedly Whitehead.

46. New York: Collier-Macmillan, 1953.

47. Hartshorne here claims that panentheism is a requirement of religion as much as of philosophy. This claim is central to his thought.

48. 'The Reality of God' (S.C.M. Press, 1967) p. 62.

49. See especially 'Philosophers Speak of God', pp. 3-6.

50. 'Reality as Social Process', p. 40.

51. 'Philosophers Speak of God', p. 10.

52. Ibid., pp. 14-15.

53. La Salle, Ill.: Open Court, 1962.

54. Admittedly Hartshorne considers this objection in his 'A Natural Theology for our Time' (La Salle Ill.: Open Court, 1967) pp. 9-12. But none of his examples (such as those of the poet creating images or a teacher being enriched by the response of his pupils) constitutes a parallel to the idea of one self including another.

55. It cannot be too strongly stressed that the doctrine of the Trinity defines the Christian understanding of God's love. For the basic principles that govern the interpretation of the doctrine I must refer the reader back to my remarks in my first section on 'Classical theism'. A full and perceptive account of recent writing on the subject is contained in C. Welch's 'The Trinity in Contemporary Theology' (S.C.M. Press, 1953).

56. 'Philosophers Speak of God', p. 162.

57. Published in the 'Proceedings of the American Catholic Philosophical Association' (Washington, 1961).

CHAPTER 3

1. 'The Idea of God in the Light of Recent Philosophy' — lectures delivered in 1912 and 1913 and published in 1920 (Oxford University Press).

2. 'The Idea of God', pp. 70 and 77. On pp. 181-2 Pringle-Pattison also rejects pan-psychism — the view that all organisms possess some form of mind.

3. The two terms are used interchangeably.

4. On p. 387 Pringle-Pattison endorses James Ward's statement that 'God is God only as being creative'.

5. 'The Idea of God', pp. 294-5.

6. This is 'the principle of contradiction' which in any case (so Pringle-Pattison urges on p. 233) does not yield the monistic conclusions that Bradley draws from it.

7. 'The Idea of God', p. 272.

8. Ibid., pp. 144 and 408.

9. Ibid., p. 410.

10. He expresses his sympathy with, and indebtedness to, Hegel at several points: see especially pp. 154, 218, 304, 312. He endorses the panentheistic elements in Hegel according to which God, though immanent in the world, also to some degree transcends it; but he explicitly repudiates the pantheistic elements in which Hegel coincides with Spinoza (p. 339).

11. I can only observe that his arguments for a teleological and metaphysical interpretation of evolution have recently been impressively corroborated by Errol Harris in his 'The Foundations of Metaphysics in Science' (Allen & Unwin, 1965).

12. 'The Idea of God', pp. 355-65.

13. Ibid., pp. 382-3, 395-6.

14. See my previous observations on Spinoza and Hampshire's account of him.

15. 'The Idea of God', pp. 339-40.

16. The error that God is *im*personal.

17. 'The Idea of God', pp. 166-8.

18. There he describes belief in the Absolute as 'a postulate of reason', 'a supreme hypothesis', 'a venture of faith'.

159

19. English trans. Edinburgh 1957. All my references (unless otherwise stated) are to this work.

20. Thus on p. 84 he describes the First Vatican Council's pronouncement on natural theology as 'wicked and damnable', and the 'god' to which every form of such theology leads as an 'idol'.

21. English trans. London 1949, pp. 35-6.

22. Barth's own doctrine of the Trinity is contained in the first volume of his 'Church Dogmatics'.

23. The essay (together with other essays by Barth) is published in English under the title 'The Humanity of God' (Collins, 1961).

24. See especially pp. 46-8.

25. 'Church Dogmatics', p. 299.

26. Ibid., pp. 287-97.

27. Barth quotes Feuerbach, but not (strangely) Freud, for this view.

28. 'Church Dogmatics', pp. 498-9.

29. Thus he writes that 'Christian faith is not irrational, but rational in the proper sense', and that 'faith means knowledge' ('Dogmatics in Outline', p. 23).

30. Thus Victor White points out that when Barth says that 'God is personal, but personal in an incomprehensible way', he is presupposing the analogy of proportionality. White further claims that the passage he quotes from Barth 'may be paralleled almost *verbatim* in Penido's treatment of the same subject' ('God the Unknown' (Harvill Press, 1956) pp. 32 and 34).

31. Eph. 3: 14-15.

32. As I have already urged, the *analogia fidei* implies the *analogia entis*; for first, God could not become Man unless there were *some* proportionality between the divine and human natures, and secondly, the very idea of a God who reveals himself implies the applicability of personal analogies to God. That all theistic discourse presupposes the *analogia entis* is conclusively shown by Brunner *contra* Barth ('Natural Theology' (London: Centenary Press, 1946) pp. 54-6).

33. I use 'saving' in the maximal sense of a knowledge that makes a person spiritually perfect and so fit for the vision of

160

God. (I should maintain strongly that all natural truth and goodness can *contribute* to such salvation.)

34. All my references (unless otherwise stated) are to the first volume of his 'Dogmatics', trans. Olive Wyon under the title 'The Christian Doctrine of God' (Lutterworth Press, 1949).

35. Ibid., p. 229.

36. Hence Brunner rejects the idea of 'double predestination'.

37. Brunner has never conceded to non-Christians any more than a vague, minimal knowledge of God. See his debate with Barth ('Natural Theology', pp. 32-3). Barth has no difficulty in showing on pp. 80-2 that even this concession is incompatible with Brunner's statements elsewhere that all natural knowledge of God is idolatrous, and that 'materially' man has entirely lost God's image through the Fall.

38. Allen & Unwin, 1927.

39. Allen & Unwin, 1956.

40. This grading is common throughout the history of Hindu thought. For another modern example, see H. D. Bhattacharya's essay in 'Radhakrishnan: Comparitive Studies in Philosophy Presented in Honour of his Sixtieth Birthday' (Allen & Unwin, 1951) pp. 211-15.

41. 'The Hindu View of Life', p. 27.

42. Ibid., pp. 67-8.

43. 'Recovery of Faith', p. 83. The reference is to Exodus 3:13-14.

44. Ibid., p. 84.

45. Italics mine.

46. 'Recovery of Faith', p. 148 (italics mine).

47. My references are to 'The Perennial Philosophy' (Chatto & Windus, 1946).

48. He quotes similar passages from Ruysbroeck, Philo and Eckhart on pp. 40-1.

49. 'The Perennial Philosophy', pp. 29-30, 62-3.

50. His failure to recognise this impossibility is further shown on pp. 67-8 of his 'The Hindu View of Life', where he praises Sankara and F. H. Bradley for remaining 'agnostic' concerning the Absolute's relation to the world. But they

were *not* agnostic. They interpreted the relation monistically.

51. Radhakrishnan underestimates the tension between monism and theism in Indian thought. On this tension, see Ninian Smart's 'Doctrine and Argument in Indian Philosophy' (Allen & Unwin, 1964).

52. Nisbet, 1953.

53. 'Systematic Theology', pp. 124-7.

54. Ibid., p. 15 (italics his).

55. Ibid., p. 17 (italics his).

56. Ibid., pp. 11-12, 80-1, 105-7.

57. For a full-scale discussion of Tillich's Christology, see George Tavard's 'Paul Tillich and the Christian Message' (Burns & Oates, 1962).

58. There are also many other valuable aspects of Tillich's thought with which I cannot deal — chiefly his idea of 'correlation', his claims for an intuitive activity of the intellect, his account of 'anxiety', his discussion of symbols, and his reflections on culture. Unfortunately I am obliged to consider his thought at its weakest points.

59. To put it in scholastic terminology, the specification of God's nature (*quid est*) through analogical predication is logically dependent on the affirmation of his existence (*quod est*).

60. In an essay contributed to 'The Theology of Paul Tillich', ed. C. W. Kegley (New York: Collier-Macmillan, 1961), Hartshorne welcomes Tillich as an exponent of 'dipolarism', but criticises him for not affirming explicitly that God is Process-itself no less than Being-itself (pp. 166 and 194). In his reply Tillich says that he is 'not disinclined to accept the process-character of being-itself' (p. 339). He adds that he feels 'a close affinity to the philosophy of religion represented by Hartshorne, perhaps because of common intellectual antecedents, for example Bergson, Schelling and Böhme' (p. 340). Yet he still fails to see the metaphysical necessity of choosing decisively between monopolar and dipolar theism.

61. 'The Systematic Theology of Paul Tillich' (Lutterworth Press, 1964) p. 126.

62. The same objection can be brought against Frederick

162

Ferré's more recent definition of religion as 'one's way of valuing most comprehensively and intensively' ('Basic Modern Philosophy of Religion' (Allen & Unwin, 1968) p. 69). On his own admission this definition would include a dogmatic form of Communism.

63. 'The Shaking of the Foundations' (S.C.M. Press, 1949) p. 57.

64. Ibid., pp. 58-9.

65. Tillich shows a closer resemblance to Radhakrishnan than to any other of the thinkers I have examined. Both divorce God's Being from his existence; both speak of God panentheistically; both regard him as overcoming non-being within his nature; both advocate a transcendental unity of religions in which the historical Jesus becomes irrevelant and in which, therefore, the distinctive claims of Christianity evaporate.

66. Darton, Longman & Todd, 1965.

67. All my references are to 'Honest to God' (S.C.M. Press, 1963).

68. Ibid., p. 132.

69. Hepburn's claim is explicitly repudiated by Robinson (pp. 40-1).

70. S.C.M. Press, 1967.

71. 'Exploration into God', pp. 55-6.

72. He fails to explain (what is surely inexplicable) how God can *act* personally without *being* personal.

73. S.C.M. Press, 1966.

74. Macquarrie expresses his indebtedness to Heidegger on p. 105. But how far his use of the term 'Being' is compatible with Heidegger's philosophy is a question that lies outside my scope and competence. Hence I shall examine Macquarrie without any reference to Heidegger.

75. 'Principles of Christian Theology', pp. 97-100.

76. See the last of his initial negative statements about 'Being'.

77. It must be noted that Macquarrie's account of divine Being forms only one chapter in part 1. Although it and the following two chapters (on theistic language and the nature of religion) are crucial they occupy only a comparatively

small part of the whole work. They are preceded (as I said earlier) by an 'existentialist' analysis of the human situation, and they are suceeded by a detailed discussion of distinctively Christian doctrines.

78. 'An Introduction to Philosophy' (Sheed & Ward, 1946) p. 145.

79. Macquarrie's account of God's relation to the world is ambiguous. On the one hand he affirms the doctrine of creation *ex nihilo* and repudiates pantheism (pp. 201-2). On the other hand he states that God 'puts himself' into the entities he creates (pp. 202 and 275); so that the world is a *substantial* 'manifestation' of God's 'presence'.

80. Strangely, he does not examine Hartshorne's dipolarism.

CONCLUSION

1. Thus I have departed from strict Thomism in my interpretations of omniscience and impassibility.

2. I must express my dissent from these thinkers. It seems to me that we cannot validly call a theological system 'Christian' if it is contrary to the basic teaching of the Bible. And there can be no doubt that the Bible excludes panentheism, pantheism, emanationism, and belief in a finite God. On the most liberal view Christianity requires belief in God as the uncreated Creator of all things.

3. Since Hartshorne finds the doctrine of divine impassibility the most objectionable element in classical theism, it is important to distinguish between the doctrine, his own view, and the view I have put forward. The doctrine affirms that God suffers in his human but not his divine nature; Hartshorne affirms that God suffers in one but not the other pole of his being; and I have affirmed that God transfigures in his changeless being the sufferings he vicariously feels. Although all these affirmations are paradoxical, only Hartshorne's involves a proposition of the type 'A is both X and not-X'.

164

4. I have given reasons for this view in my 'The Moral Argument for Christian Theism' (Allen & Unwin, 1965).

5. For a statement of the general principles that ought to govern our understanding of this doctrine, I must refer the reader back to my first section on theism. It may be objected that even if the basic affirmations of Christian theism are not self-contradictory, this doctrine is so. Admittedly the doctrine is the most paradoxical of Christian beliefs concerning God's nature. Admittedly too it is a paradox that is bound to seem intolerable to a non-Christian who does not share the Scriptural insights from which it stems and by which alone it is justified. And I cannot examine either these insights or the Church's development of them within the limits of this book. But there is no contradiction in supposing that an infinite being could express his nature in a life of mutual love. On the contrary such a life, though a complete mystery to finite minds, would represent the perfection of selfhood. Paul Henry states it thus: 'God is the perfect, in fact the only perfect, prototype of that which all love between persons tends to achieve — absolute unity and yet distinction — to be one with the other, not by losing one's identity but by perfecting it, even at the very source of one's being. That is why divine existence is the ideal of all personal existence — to be fully oneself, but only in dependence upon, and in adherence to, another in the communion of unity' ('St Augustine on Personality' (New York: Collier-Macmillan, 1960)).

6. I have given my own analysis of faith and its grounds in my 'The Christian Knowledge of God' (Athlone Press, 1969).

Select Bibliography

(Works by and on the writers discussed in Chapter 3 are omitted.)

General

E. O. James, 'Concepts of Deity' (Hutchinson, 1950).

R. Otto, 'The Idea of the Holy', trans. J. W. Harvey (Oxford University Press, 1925).

J. Oman, 'The Natural and the Supernatural' (Cambridge University Press, 1931).

R. C. Zaehner, 'The Catholic Church and World Religions' (Burns & Oates, 1964).

'The Supreme Reality in Non-Christian Religions' ('Studia Missionalia', XVII, Rome: Gregorian University Press, 1968).

N. Smart, 'Reasons and Faiths' (Routledge & Kegan Paul, 1958).

A. C. Bouquet, 'Comparative Religion' (Penguin Books, 1951).

'Encyclopedia of Religion and Ethics' (article on 'Theism').

'Encyclopedia of Philosophy' (articles on 'God', 'Infinity' and 'Theism').

'New Catholic Encyclopedia' (article on 'God').

'Philosophers Speak of God', an anthology ed. Charles Hartshorne and William L. Reese (University of Chicago Press, 1953).

F. C. Copleston, 'A History of Philosophy' (Burns & Oates, 1946–).

H. R. Mackintosh, 'Types of Modern Theology' (Fontana ed., 1964).

John Macquarrie, 'Twentieth-Century Religious Thought' (S.C.M. Press, 1963).

J. Collins, 'God in Modern Philosophy' (Chicago: Regnery, 1959).

Thomas J. J. Altizer and William Hamilton, 'Radical Theology and the Death of God' (Penguin Books, 1968).

David Jenkins, 'Guide to the Debate about God' (Lutterworth Press, 1966).

H. Zahrnt, 'The Question of God: Protestant Theology in the Twentieth Century' (Collins, 1969).

John Baillie, 'The Idea of Revelation in Recent Thought' (Oxford University Press, 1956).

Primitive religions

M. Eliade, 'Patterns in Comparative Religion' (Sheed & Ward, 1958).

Evans Pritchard, 'Theories of Primitive Religion' (Oxford University Press, 1965).

Ancient Greek religion

Gilbert Murray, 'Five Stages of Greek Religion' (Watts, 1943).

W. K. Guthrie, 'The Greeks and their Gods' (Methuen, 1950).

Ancient Near Eastern religions

E. O. James, 'The Ancient Gods' (Weidenfeld & Nicolson, 1960).

Hinduism

R. C. Zaehner, 'Hinduism' (Oxford University Press, 1962).

N. Smart, 'Doctrine and Argument in Indian Philosophy' (Allen & Unwin, 1964).

Islam

Louis Gardet, 'Les grandes problèmes de la théologie musulmane' (Paris: Vrin, 1967).

Judaism

Walther Eichrodt, 'Theology of the Old Testament', English trans. vols 1 and 2 (S.C.M. Press, 1961 and 1967).

J. Bonsirven, 'Palestinian Judaism in the Time of Jesus Christ' (Holt, Rinehart & Winston, New York, 1964).

H. A. Wolfson, 'Philo', 2 vols (Cambridge, Mass., 1947).

Christianity (see also under *Theism*)

'The New Testament Background: Selected Documents', ed. C. K. Barrett (S.P.C.K., 1956).

R. Bultmann, 'Primitive Christianity in its Contemporary Setting' (Thames & Hudson, 1956).

A. W. Argyle, 'God in the New Testament' (Hodder & Stoughton, 1965).

Alan Richardson, 'An Introduction to the Theology of the New Testament' (S.C.M. Press, 1958).

Karl Rahner, 'Theological Investigations', I (Darton, Longman & Todd, 1961): the essay entitled 'Theos in the New Testament', pp. 79-148.

G. L. Prestige, 'God in Patristic Thought' (Heinemann, 1963).

J. N. D. Kelly, 'Early Christian Doctrines' (Black, 1960).

'An Augustine Synthesis', passages in English translation arranged by E. Przywara (Sheed & Ward, 1945).

Thomas Aquinas, 'Summa Theologica' 1a 1-49, Latin text and English translation in vols 1-8 of the Blackfriars ed. (London: Eyre & Spottiswoode, and New York: Mcgraw-Hill, 1964−).

Thomas Aquinas, 'Philosophical Texts' and 'Theological Texts', an anthology in English by Thomas Gilby (Oxford University Press, 1951 and 1955).

168

R. L. Patterson, 'The Conception of God in the Philosophy of Aquinas' (Allen & Unwin, 1933).

F. C. Copleston, 'Aquinas' (Penguin Books, 1955).

Duns Scotus, 'A Treatise on God as First Principle', trans. and ed. Allen B. Woolter (Chicago: Franciscan Herald Press, 1966).

John Calvin, 'Institutes of the Christian Religion', bks 1 and 2, trans. Henry Beveridge, I (James Clarke, 1949).

Classical theism

R. Garrigou-Lagrange, 'God his Existence and Nature', trans. Bede Rose, 2 vols (St Louis: Herder, 1934).

E. Gilson, 'God and Philosophy' (Yale University Press, 1941).

——, 'The Elements of Christian Philosophy' (Mentor-Omega Books, New American Library, 1960).

F. Von Hügel, 'Essays and Addresses on the Philosophy of Religion', 2 vols (Dent, 1921 and 1926).

A. M. Farrer, 'Finite and Infinite' (Dacre Press, 1943).

E. L. Mascall, 'He Who Is' (Longmans, Green, 1945).

——, 'Existence and Analogy' (Longmans, Green, 1949).

T. Gornall, 'A Philosophy of God' (Darton, Longman & Todd, 1962).

F. Van Steenberghen, 'The Hidden God' (Herder, 1966).

V. Preller, 'Divine Science and the Science of God' (Princeton University Press, 1967).

C. S. Lewis, 'Mere Christianity' (Fontana ed., 1963).

Theism in general

C. Webb, 'God and Personality' (Allen & Unwin, 1918).

W. Temple, 'Nature, Man and God' (Macmillan, 1934–).

W. R. Matthews, 'God in Christian Thought and Experience' (Nisbet, 1930).

F. R. Tennant, 'Philosophical Theology', II (Cambridge University Press, 1930).

E. Bevan, 'Symbolism and Belief' (Allen & Unwin, 1938).

J. Laird, 'Theism and Cosmology' (Allen & Unwin, 1940).

——, 'Mind and Deity' (Allen & Unwin, 1941).

G. F. Stout, 'God and Nature' (Cambridge University Press, 1952).

H. H. Farmer, 'God and Men' (Nisbet, 1948).

W. G. Maclagan, 'The Theological Frontier of Ethics' (Allen & Unwin, 1961).

C. A. Campbell, 'Selfhood and Godhood' (Allen & Unwin, 1957).

The concept of a finite God

A. E. Taylor, 'A Commentary on Plato's Timaeus' (Oxford University Press, 1928).

F. M. Cornford, 'Plato's Cosmology', a translation of and commentary on Plato's 'Timaeus' (Kegan Paul, 1937).

J. S. Mill, 'Theism', edited with an introduction by Richard Taylor (New York: Bobbs-Merrill, 1957).

A. N. Whitehead, 'Science and the Modern World' (Cambridge University Press, 1926).

E. S. Brightman, 'The Problem of God' (New York: Abingdon Press, 1930).

The Neo-Platonic concept of God

'The Enneads of Plotinus', trans. Stephen MacKenna, revised by B. S. Page and introduced by Paul Henry (Faber, 1956).

E. R. Dodds, 'Select Passages Illustrating Neo-Platonism' (S.P.C.K., 1923).

W. R. Inge, 'The Philosophy of Plotinus', 2 vols (Longmans, 1918).

A. H. Armstrong, 'Architecture of the Intelligible Universe in the Philosophy of Plotinus' (Cambridge University Press, 1940).

Pantheism and monism

Edwyn Bevan, 'Stoics and Sceptics' (Oxford University Press, 1913).

Marcus Aurelius, 'Meditations', ed. with translation and commentary by A. S. L. Farquharson, 2 vols (Oxford University Press, 1944).

Spinoza, 'Ethics', trans. Andrew Boyle (Everyman's Library, Dent, 1959).

S. Hampshire, 'Spinoza' (Penguin Books, 1951).

Hegel, 'The Phenomenology of Mind', trans. J. Baillie, 2nd ed. (Allen & Unwin, 1949).

E. Caird, 'Hegel' (Edinburgh and London: Blackwood, 1911).

Josiah Royce, 'The Conception of God' (New York: Macmillan, 1898).

F. H. Bradley, 'Appearance and Reality' (Oxford University Press, 1897).

Henry Jones, 'A Faith that Enquires' (Macmillan, 1922).

W. T. Stace, 'Mysticism and Philosophy' (Macmillan, 1961).

Process theology

A. N. Whitehead, 'Process and Reality' (Cambridge University Press, 1929).

Charles Hartshorne, 'The Divine Relativity' (Yale University Press, 1948).

——, 'The Logic of Perfection' (La Salle, Ill.: Open Court, 1962).

——, 'Reality as Social Process' (New York: Collier-Macmillan, 1963).

——, 'Man's Vision of God' (New York: Harper, 1941).

Schubert Ogden, 'The Reality of God' (New York: Harper & Row, 1961; London: S.C.M. Press, 1967).

John B. Cobb, 'A Christian Natural Theology' (Philadelphia: Westminste. Press, 1965; London: Lutterworth Press, 1966).

Stephen Ely, 'The Religious Availability of Whitehead's God' (University of Wisconsin Press, 1942).

D. D. Williams, 'The Spirit and the Forms of Love' (Nisbet, 1968).

'Process and Divinity: Philosophical Essays presented to Charles Hartshorne' (La Salle, Ill.: Open Court, 1964).

N. Pittenger, 'Process-Thought and Christian Faith' (Nisbet, 1968).

Index

Date Due

OCT 24 '79			
AUG 28 '85			